AZALEA TAILOR

Becoming Her. Becoming Me.

For every woman who lost herself trying to be everything to everyone... and finally chose to be herself.

the female
COLLECTIVE

First published by The Female Collective 2025

First edition

ISBN: 978-1-9192696-0-3

This book was professionally typeset on Reedsy.
Find out more at reedsy.com

This book was written by one woman but carries the fingerprints of many. To every woman who shaped me – through love, loss and the lessons life demanded. My grandmother, who taught me strength wrapped in softness. My mother, who showed me how to live life on my own terms – unapologetically, fiercely, and without waiting for permission. My sisters, who never let me fall without reminding me how to stand again. And my gorgeous niece, who reminded me how to love with a wide-open heart.

Acknowledgments

This book may have been written in solitude, but it was carried into the world by the hands, hearts, and patience of many.

To my sisters – Anita, Narinder, Krishma and my sister in law, Vickee. Thank you for being there from the very beginning. Not just for your thoughtful feedback, but for helping me choose the title, the strapline, even the cover. Your instincts and encouragement have been my compass throughout this journey.

To my family who I'd choose as friends time and time again – My beautiful aunt Darshan, and my cousins - Reet, Laal, Nil and Shorty. Your unwavering support and belief in me has meant more than I could ever put into words. Thank you for always cheering me on, near or far.

To my brothers – Tej, Tony, Kam and Kishan. Thank you for believing in me, even if you had no idea what I was actually writing. For reminding me, in your own ways, that I was always capable, even when I doubted it. Your quiet pride, your teasing, your presence, they all meant more than you know.

To my friends – Clive, Sue and Steph. Thank you for your grace, your space, and your understanding while I locked myself away, head down in rewrites and word counts. Your patience, even in my absence, reminded me that true friendships hold firm through every season.

To my cheeky proofreader – Robski. Thank you for your eagle eyes and mischief. You made the commas less painful, and the process far more fun. You caught what I couldn't.

To my chum from another mum – Trace. Thank you for lending me Momma Bear and gifting me the kind of feedback every writer dreams of – thoughtful, honest and instinctive. You helped me get it right before I sent it out into the world.

And finally, to my darling nieces – Maya and Ayva, and my adorable nephews – Aman, Arjie, Kavi and Jayden. Thank you for being my why. You are the reason I wrote this, and the reminder that the stories we pass down matter just as much as the ones we live. You inspired me to tell the truth, and to do it bravely.

This book may be mine in voice, but it's ours in spirit.

Thank you for standing beside me while I turned my story into something that could hold others.

PROLOGUE _THE MAKING OF ME

We don't get to choose who we become – not at first. Before we start carving out who we are, we inherit, and we absorb. We sponge up everything around us. The laughter. The silences. The chaos. The calm. The moods in the room. The way our parents speak to each other (or don't). The way our mothers navigate life with silent strength and perfectly timed sighs. The way our fathers try to protect us from a world they're still trying to figure out themselves. And the stories told on loop by the elders who walked before us – stories that stretch back to places we've never been, with people we'll never meet, but who somehow live inside us anyway. Childhood isn't just a chapter. It's the blueprint. The scaffolding. The silent architect of everything we'll become.

I was born long before I knew how to wear my own skin.

Back then, '*me*' was an echo – a half-drawn sketch stitched together with my great-grandfather's tales of life in Africa, biscuit crumbs from the tin he kept under lock and key, and the unmistakable rhythm of my mother's voice bouncing down the hallway when dinner was ready, or someone was in trouble (*usually me*).

I grew up in a house that buzzed with life. One of those full-fat family homes where every bedroom told a different story. Four generations under one roof. Aunts. Uncles. Cousins. Noise. Love. And a rotating cast of slippers and advice. Privacy was a luxury. Personal space? A myth. But somehow, that house taught me everything about connection – how to live together, how to fight fair (*or not*), how to be heard even when no one was listening.

And me? I was the eldest. Spoiled? Probably. Loved? Fiercely.

I sat on laps instead of sofas. Held instead of hushed. I was wrapped in love and laced with cheek. Sugar on the outside. Spark on the inside.

But boy, was I defiant, even as a little girl, I knew how to manipulate the meaning of a sentence to suit me. If I was told to change out of my school uniform, I did – into something new my mother had bought for me. Was she impressed? Absolutely not. Could she argue with my logic? Not one bit.

That was me – a boundary tester with a beautiful bob and Mary Jane shoes.

A girl who used to think that becoming yourself was something that just... happened. Like one day, you'd wake up, throw back the duvet, and boom – there you'd be. Complete. Fully formed. *That girl*. The one who knows where she's going. The one with answers, red lips, and a Pinterest-worthy life plan. The one who doesn't lose her keys or cry over silly things or second-guess every life decision.

But the truth? Becoming me wasn't a moment. It was a process.

A slow burn. Not a dramatic entrance, but a quiet unfolding. A messy mosaic made up of half-heard compliments, whispered insecurities, wrong turns, right instincts, and more than a few nights staring at the ceiling asking myself *"Is this it?"*

And there were times when everything had to fall apart before I could feel even remotely put together.

Becoming me wasn't about becoming someone new. It was about remembering who I already was – underneath the noise, the masks, and the expectations.

It was about reclaiming the little girl who ran across the road in her school shoes, breathless and free, knowing exactly how late she could be without getting into trouble.

So, this is the prologue:
To the woman I am now.
To the girl I once was.
To the many versions of me in between.

- The one with the big personality and even bigger dreams.
- The one who had no idea where she was going – only that it had to be somewhere more beautiful, more freeing, more *her* than where she began.

My story doesn't start with a grand revelation. It starts in shared bedrooms filled with whispered secrets and stolen moments of stillness. In playgrounds where I learned to laugh at the right jokes, and how to use humour as armour. In mirrors where I practised being someone worth liking – before I realised the only person I really needed to like me... *was me*.

It starts with little girl me, wild-hearted and soft-souled.

A girl who loved too hard, felt too deeply, and believed grown-ups had it all figured out (*spoiler alert: they don't*). Most of them still don't.

I was a child full of questions:

Why do people lie?
Why do girls have to be nice?
Why do adults find love so hard, when children give unconditional love so easily?
Are relationships always destined to break?
And the question I carried around like a secret – *Why does confidence fit everyone else like a tailored suit, and me like an itchy jumper with the label still in?*

The earliest version of me was contradiction in motion – shy in one breath, bossy in the next. A quiet storm with a loud heart.

I was one of those girls who looked like she floated through life with polished hair and perfect poise – but was all elbows and ambition. Always two steps behind but ten dreams ahead.

It took me a while to realise – who we are isn't something we find once and for all. It's something we uncover, layer by layer, moment by moment. It's in the way we love. The way we rise. The way we fall apart and piece ourselves back together.

We inherit parts of ourselves, yes. But we also get to rewrite the parts that no longer fit.

So, if you're looking for a beginning, this is mine. Not a fairytale. Not a warning. Just a girl, in a house full of people, trying to figure out who she is.

A girl with questions – a big heart, and drive.
A girl who didn't glide – she climbed.
A girl who didn't bloom overnight – *she blossomed in chapters.*

And if you're still becoming you, I promise – you're not late.

You're right on time.

I

HOW I BECAME ME

Every version of me started here. In chaos. In comfort. In rooms where love didn't always sound like 'I love you' but it showed up anyway.

I didn't become me gently. I was built in the noise. By sharp tongues and warm hugs. By rules that changed with moods. By women who carried too much but never dropped the ball.

I grew up learning how to read a room before I could read a book. How to keep the peace and secrets that weren't mine. It's where I learned loyalty before language, resilience before reason, and how to hold it all together, even when no one told me I had to.

This was my beginning – the unfiltered, unpolished, unforgettable start of me.

1

WHERE IT ALL BEGAN FOR ME

Grandparents are proof that love doesn't follow rules or wear a watch. It lives in a warm lap. In a well-worn story, told for the hundredth time because they know you need it. In a cupboard with a tin of forbidden treats. In the smell of Tiger Balm and the sound of gold bangles. In laughter that fills a house and silence that holds you steady. Their love is simple. The kind that roots you and lives in your bones long after they're gone. A love that teaches you – this is where you began and this is who you are.

I didn't just grow up with grandparents – I hit the generational jackpot. Most kids knew their grandmother as the lady who wore floral dresses and made questionable rice pudding. But me? I had front-row seats to a full-blown dynasty. Grandparents and great-grandparents. It was like growing up in a living museum of wisdom, wit, and wobbly furniture.

While other children were still trying to pronounce '*Nana.*' I was fluent in the sacred language of four o'clock stories, cupboard-guarded treats, and ancestral truths disguised as bedtime tales.

It wasn't just a childhood; it was a multi-generational mash-up of mayhem, morals, and magical stories.

We were a house full of characters – a sitcom waiting to happen. Crammed into a four-bedroom house bursting at the seams with people, noise, and secrets. There was my grandmother, my mum and dad, my two uncles, my aunt, my five siblings... and reigning over us all, with velvet authority, and a little help from my great-grandmother – my great-grandfather. It was chaos. The kind of chaos that undoubtedly shapes you without asking for your permission.

You couldn't take a single step without bumping into someone, physically or emotionally. Our house was like a beehive – busy, buzzing, occasionally stinging, but always alive. Privacy was a luxury. If you managed to sneak into the bathroom without a knock or a *"How long you gonna be?"* you were basically royalty. But in that madness was magic. Somehow, in the whirlwind of it all, there was deep, grounding love.

My great-grandfather was the lead actor in our family drama. He didn't just tell stories – he was the story. A man with a booming voice, regal posture, and a stare so sharp it could slice through the Sunday roast (well, at least I know where I get it from). His word wasn't just respected – it was law. Challenging him was like arguing with a thunderstorm – you could try, but you'd end up soaked and sorry.

Every day, like clockwork, the ritual began – four o'clock sharp. My siblings and I would abandon whatever mischief we were in the middle of, sprint up the stairs, and burst into his room without knocking. You didn't need permission to enter when you were summoned by greatness. We'd take our seats on the floor like loyal disciples. Legs crossed. Eyes wide. Ears tingling – and wait for the magic to begin.

And oh, the stories. They weren't just tales – they were transport systems. One minute we were in rainy Scotland, the next, knee-deep in red African dust, chasing elephants, dodging lions, and learning the difference between bravery and foolishness. His voice rose and fell like waves, thick with accents and layered with humour. Every parable ended with a life lesson – some subtle, others not so much. *"Your dad and uncles would quiver in their boots, but your aunt, she was a true lioness,"* he'd say with a wink. *"Always remember – nothing scares us.. We're a family of lions. We're born to rule."*

He painted with words – broad, bold strokes that coloured our imaginations. We didn't need books when we had him. His stories didn't just entertain, they instilled. Values. Courage. Identity. He could stretch a five-minute story into an hour-long odyssey, all without ever needing to check the time. We were riveted. There was not a chance in hell we were going to interrupt.

Nestled behind the door of a tall, mysterious cupboard that stood guard like a sentinel was an old SMA baby formula tin. From the outside, it looked unimpressive. But inside? Treasure. Treats. Forbidden fruit – pink wafer biscuits, rock sugar sweets, and fox nuts. The fact that it lived next to his beloved shotgun, his favourite three-piece suit, and his sheepskin coat only added to the mystique. The cupboard wasn't just furniture

– it was an altar. And that tin? Our holy grail.

But woe betide anyone who dared to open it without his permission. One cousin tried once. Let's just say he still twitches when he hears the words, "*Who wants a treat?*"

There was structure in his sternness. Power in his pauses. And love, always love – even if it came dressed as discipline. He didn't raise his voice unless absolutely necessary, but when he did, even the walls quivered. Yet in the quiet moments, the cracks showed. The softening of his features when my great-grandmother walked into the room. The way he adjusted himself. Straightened up before she entered – like a schoolboy caught daydreaming. You could see the outline of love, decades deep.

She was his anchor. His queen. His match in every way. Quietly formidable. Fiercely adored. She never challenged him in public, not that she needed to. Behind closed doors, we knew who really wore the trousers. And he? He wouldn't dare breathe sideways without checking she was okay with it. Their relationship was a masterclass in partnership – fiery, funny, occasionally farcical, but always fused with love and respect.

When he told a story, she'd sit on her bed, hands clasped, listening like it was the first time – even though it was probably the fiftieth. And when he delivered the punchline, she would throw her head back and laugh, so deeply that tears rolled down her cheeks. It was the kind of love that made the air feel warmer. And for me, it set a bar so high that my adult relationships have spent a lifetime trying to reach.

She had her own stories too. Less dramatic, more deliberate. While he took you on wild adventures, she'd lull you into quiet reflection. Her stories came with simmering pots and softly spoken truths, often delivered while he took a break, because my sister was combing his hair. Together, they were the perfect contrast – fire and water, storm and stillness.

I didn't realise it then, but those afternoons were sacred. More than just tales, they were transmissions. His stories didn't just entertain, they educated. They preserved our heritage. Stitched it into our skin like fine embroidery. Through him, I learned that to tell your story is to own your identity. That your past isn't just something you walk away from – it's something you carry with grace and a side of humour.

It's where I first learned to listen. Not just hear – really listen. To the spaces between the words. The rhythm in the silences. I learned that sometimes, the most important things aren't said outright. They're implied. Hinted at. Wrapped in metaphor. He taught me that every story has power – even the messy ones *(especially the messy ones)*.

He passed that power on to me – along with the biscuits, the side eye, and the occasional reluctant hug. I inherited it like a birthright, one that came wrapped in silk and smelled faintly of TCP and Tiger Balm. Looking back, I see now how those early years were more than just foundational – they were formational. I didn't just inherit DNA, I inherited a legacy. And while I might have been the cheeky girl sneaking out the back door for unsanctioned adventures, I was also a sponge, soaking up every bit of history, love, and chaos around me.

If my great-grandfather was the storyteller, the showman, the thunderclap that echoed through our home, then my grandmother *(his daughter-in-law)* was the stillness that followed the storm. The quiet hum beneath the chaos. The woman who held it all together, even when everything threatened to fall apart. She wasn't loud. She didn't need to be. Her silence spoke volumes. She moved through our home like a force of nature wrapped in cotton suits. Unapologetic. Unshakable. Always ten steps ahead of whatever disaster was about to unfold – whether it was a burnt curry, a scraped knee, or a full-blown family feud.

To the untrained eye, she might have looked like just another matriarch. But to me, she was a miracle worker in slippers. A woman who could settle an argument with a single look. Who would sew into the early hours, massage oil into our hair, make twenty rotis without breaking a sweat – and still have time to iron a week's worth of uniforms while saying her daily prayers.

Her strength wasn't the kind that shouted from rooftops – it was the kind that built the damn roof in the first place.

Her life was all about sacrifice. Always in motion. Sewing. Massaging. Ironing. Folding clothes with a precision the army would envy. And when those hands touched you, it felt like being grounded. The world could be crumbling, but if she had you in her arms, you'd survive it – because she had you. She had each and every one of us.

I used to think she had a sixth sense. She always knew who needed what, before they did. She was always doing, always giving, and she never asked for anything in return. Not once. She was the middle layer in our multi-generational sandwich – tucked between the towering authority of my great-grandfather and the messy ambition of her children. She carried the weight of two generations on her back and never once let it break her. That's resilience. That's love.

Looking back, I honestly don't know how she did it. Four children of her own. Ten grandchildren running riot. A house that never stayed clean for longer than five minutes... and yet, she never faltered. She was like Superwoman – only she didn't need a cape. Just a strong cup of chai and a quiet moment at the sewing machine to gather her thoughts. She walked with such purpose – no dithering, no dragging of feet, just a full on march. Her fur-lined slippers smacking the floor with intent. She had places to be. People to see. Laundry to sort.

Frugal? Absolutely. But make no mistake – she was no miser. She was a magician with a budget. Leftovers weren't sad in her kitchen – they were celebrated. That odd bit of dhal from the night before? Reinvented. A scrap of fabric? Transformed into something useful. Watching her, I learned that true abundance has less to do with what you have, and everything to do with how you use it. She could stretch a pound further than the bank ever could. She made ordinary things extraordinary.

My grandmother had this incredible way of keeping everyone in line without ever raising her voice. She was the queen of subtle discipline. A loud sigh. A perfectly arched brow. The pause just before she said your name in full – first, middle, and surname. That was enough. You'd be apologising before she even opened her mouth. But never in public, never in front of others. She gave you dignity, even in your wrongdoing. Her disappointment was like a mirror – silent, but utterly sobering.

One sunny day as we were driving down the motorway, just the two of us. I was going a little faster than I should have been. She kept glancing at the speedometer and when she realised I wasn't taking the hint, she very quietly said, *"This is a car, not a plane."* I smiled, took my foot off the accelerator. No argument. She had spoken and it was my job was to listen.

And yet, her laughter, oh, that laughter, it could fill the entire house. Rich. Rolling. And often at our expense. Like the time four-year-old me innocently told her, *"Don't worry Gran, I'll make you a cup of tea when you die."* She found it hysterical. She laughed so hard she had to hold her sides. That laugh was medicine. It made the walls vibrate and the chaos feel like home. It reminded us that she wasn't just the glue – she was the glitter, the spark and the soul.

As I grew older, I started to see her not just as my gran, but as the strong woman she was. A woman who had lost her husband early on in their marriage and left everything she knew behind to start again in a new country. Who learned to navigate a culture that didn't always welcome her. Who raised her children with iron in her spine and softness in her eyes. She lived through it all. Loss. Loneliness. Longing – and never once did she let the cracks show. Or if they did, she turned them into mosaic tiles and carried on.

She never complained. Not once. Even when she was tired. Even when life was unfair. She just... got on with it. She didn't crumble. She couldn't. There wasn't time – and even if there was, she'd rather pray it out than cry it out. She held everyone and everything together, and somehow made it look easy. I never once felt like I was too much for her. Too loud. Too cheeky. Too emotional. I was just *me* – and that was enough for her. She saw us all, for who we were and who we were trying to be. She was proud of us even when we weren't proud of ourselves. She was our sanctuary. The place we always came back to.

When she passed away, it felt like the sun had set on an entire universe. The house was quieter. The air heavier. Her absence wasn't just felt – it was heard. In the silence where her slippers used to scuff. In the gaps where her voice used to hum. But even in that silence, she remained. In the way we fold towels. In the way we make tea. In the way we love fiercely, quietly, without conditions. She didn't just raise children. She raised generations. She built foundations. She left footprints so deep they shaped the way we walk through life. I see her in my stubbornness; my scathing sarcasm; my laughter; my love of family and my belief that strength isn't always loud.

People often ask me where I get my resilience from. Where my backbone was built. I just smile. Because I know the answer has always been, and will always be, the same – *her*.

My childhood wasn't quiet. It wasn't tidy. It wasn't anything like the picture-perfect postcards I saw in storybooks. But it was rich – in culture, in character, in contradictions. I grew up in a house where curry simmered next to home-made fish and chips, and where discipline was dealt in hard stares and soft hands (*sometimes the other way round*).

Every object in our house held a story. The chipped teacups. The half-naked lady in the picture frame. The home-made sofa covers my grandmother lovingly sewed. Nothing matched, but everything mattered. We didn't have designer furniture, but we had furniture laced with memories. Sofas that had absorbed generations of laughter, armrests worn smooth from endless elbows during arguments, kids jumping, hugs, and stolen naps.

Even now, years later, I can still hear the soundtrack of that house – the clatter of pans' the hum of the sewing machine; the rattle of gold bangles; the crescendo of voices arguing over tea that was either too strong or not strong enough; the smell of incense mingling with fried onions. The tick of the old grandfather clock that never quite kept time – but always knew when it was story hour.

And somehow, through all the noise, tradition, and tangled relationships, I found *me* – or at least the blueprint of who I might become. It all began with those stories. With that man. That cupboard. That tin of treats. Because sometimes, becoming yourself doesn't start with a mirror. It starts with a floor. A storyteller. And the feeling that you're part of something bigger. Something older. Something beautiful.

And I can honestly say – *they were the happiest days of my life.*

The only time I truly felt free.

* * *

THE LESSONS I CARRY WITH ME

1. ***Our childhood shapes who we are:*** We don't get to choose what we absorb. Every word, every silence, every story and stare lays the foundation of who we first become.
2. ***Respect isn't taught, it's felt:*** In a glance. In a tone. In a room gone quiet. Sometimes the deepest lessons are the ones that don't use words at all.
3. ***A strong woman doesn't raise her voice, she raises generations:*** Real strength is legacy – measured by how many carry your lessons long after you've stopped giving them.
4. ***Before you can find your voice, you must learn to listen:*** Listening births empathy. It teaches us to understand the world before shaping it with our own truth.
5. ***Never let an outsider infiltrate your inner circle:*** No matter what happens behind closed doors, to the outside world, always present a united front. The moment you allow another to breach that circle, you invite chaos.

And one more truth: The love we witness in childhood shapes the love we later accept. My great-grandparents' love taught me to hold out for more – a love that laughs with you, listens to you, and lifts you, even in silence.

2

BETWEEN MUM, DAD AND ME

It takes a village to raise a child, but a child only gets one childhood. And how that village shows up – how it loves, listens, and leads, leaves fingerprints on everything that child becomes. The way they love. The way they trust. The way they feel about themselves. The way they see the world. It all starts there.

I was lucky. Blessed, really. I didn't just grow up with two parents, I grew up in a village of parental figures.

My mum and my aunt *(Nancy)* – two women under one roof, gave me double the love and, without question, double the telling offs. My other aunt, my Puwa *(Cherry)*, practically raised me. She was all softness and structure. The one who'd have snacks waiting and a long list of household chores when you got there. She even had my friends calling her Puwa and cleaning her windows when they came round. Then there was my dad, who adored me with that quiet, unwavering kind of love. And my uncle *(Taff)*, who never let me sit on the sofa alone but challenged me every step of the way.

With that village came richness. A childhood full of overlapping personalities, loud rooms, rotating rules, and love that looked different in every direction. It wasn't perfect – far from it, but it was full. And sometimes, you realise a little too late in life that full is more than enough.

Let me introduce you to my mum – a woman who wore far too much jewellery and even more confidence. She didn't just walk into a room; she made an entrance. Blind as a bat. Loud. Full of opinions. Always overdressed, and entirely unapologetic. She lived life by her own rules and wore more sparkle than a Christmas tree. If you were talking to her about something she didn't like, she'd pretend she couldn't hear you. But start gossiping in another room and she'd catch every single word. She was dramatic. Messy. Unfiltered. But always fierce and unforgettable. When she loved you, it was loud and bold. She never did anything by halves.

Then there was Nancy, married to my dad's younger brother Jas. She lived in our full-fat house and was very much my second mum. There were six of us kids, and she gave each of us the same kind of love and discipline you'd expect from a mother. Her and my mum were seamless – cooking, cleaning, sewing, bathing and raising a small army. Where one ended and the other began, no one could tell. If my mum was all fire and spice, she was sugar and ice. Structured. Warm. But never overbearing.

Cherry, my dad's sister, was the woman who prepared me for the parts of growing up no one else wanted to talk about. She taught me about periods, bras, deodorant, and even boys –

the girly stuff that needed a soft landing. Her house was my sanctuary. I'd go there before I even thought about going home. We'd eat together, me and my two cousins, and God forbid there were peas on my plate, under the table they went. She always found them later, rolled her eyes and muttered something under her breath, but I always knew I was forgiven. She made love feel simple. Never withheld. Never heavy.

My dad was my north star – charming, generous to a fault, and the kind of man who would give you the last fiver in his pocket without hesitation. He was softly spoken but magnetic, the kind of man you couldn't stay mad at even if you tried. He didn't need many words. His love was shown through actions. Through presence. Through the way he shielded me from things that might hurt. To the world, he was kind. To me, he was home.

And Taff, my dad's youngest brother – my unexpected shadow. Equal parts teddy bear and Sergeant Major. I was perched on his lap one minute and grilled on my times tables the next. He had a way of instilling discipline that put the fear of God into anyone who experienced it. He believed in respect. Routine. High expectations. But he also made sure I felt adored. He reminded me that love didn't have to look soft, to be safe.

They each gave me something different – a piece of the puzzle that made me who I am. But love, even in abundance, can't always fix what's broken at the centre. Because at the heart of that vibrant, overlapping village were my parents. And theirs was a love story that didn't end in a fairytale. It ended in deathly stares, deafening silences, and cold cups of tea left untouched.

I don't quite remember when they stopped loving each other, but even a blind person could see it. One minute they were wrapped in affection, the next they could barely exist in the same room. And yet, they stayed together. For over fifty years. Fifty years of eye rolls. Icy silences. Flared tempers. Resigned sighs. Why? Because that's what their generation was taught to do. You stuck it out. You gritted your teeth. You stayed – no matter the cost.

Growing up in that house, I made myself a silent promise – I would never accept a love like that. When it was time to leave, I'd walk away, head held high, dignity intact. Did I always follow through? Of course not. I'm human and flawed, just like the next person. I stayed too long in places I should've left. Tried to fix what was never mine to mend. But with every misstep, I learnt. I left a little sooner the next time and each time after. Because my great-grandparents showed me what love could look like – generous, joyful, whole. And my parents showed me what it should never become. I'd seen the blueprint of dysfunction, and I refused to build my life around it.

I was the firstborn to my parents, but third in line when it came to the grandchildren. Not quite the trailblazer, but definitely the one who made the most noise without saying a word. We were a close-knit tribe, squeezed into that four-bedroom house like mismatched Tupperware, full and bursting with stories, secrets, and second helpings. Privacy was mythical. Silence meant trouble. If the house was quiet, something was burning – or someone was.

I thrived in the mayhem. Self-appointed ringleader, armed

with a plan, a pout, and just enough charm to talk my way out of trouble. I wasn't loud in the obvious way, but I had a knack for mischief you couldn't quite pin on me. My calling card? Letting myself out the back door and wandering off wherever I pleased. No permission. No supervision. No apologies. To this day, freedom smells like a garden gate swinging shut behind me.

Of course they always found me – breathless and borderline smug. Half told off, half laughed at. Because deep down, they knew I was born to roam. Even if it was just to the corner shop. I wasn't rebellious, I was curious. Bold. A little too enchanted by the outside world. And maybe that was the first clue, that even in a house bursting at the seams, I was already carving out a story that belonged entirely to me.

I was daddy's girl. My father may have stopped loving my mum, but he loved me in abundance. He didn't always say it, but I knew. I felt it in the way he looked at me like I was the centre of his universe. I saw it in the way he provided. Protected. Placed me firmly above the line of fire. He made sure no harm ever came to me – not even from my mum's habit of raising her ring-clad hand before explaining why. He was my protector, my gentle giant. Quiet. Measured. Deliberate. His presence alone could calm any storm. He never raised his voice; his silence carried weight. He'd come home from work, tired and dusty, and still scoop me up like I was made of clouds. That warmth, his shoulder, his arms – they were the safest space I knew. It's something I've searched for my whole life in another.

My mum's love was... different. More complicated. She didn't like me being daddy's girl. I think, in some ways, she envied our bond – not because she didn't have her own, but because somewhere along the way, theirs had unravelled, and I'd inherited the best bits of him. Her discipline came first. A sharp word. A quicker hand. The explanation would follow after. But despite that, she loved me in her own unique way, with style, flair, and attention to detail. I always had the best haircuts, the prettiest dresses, the shiniest shoes. I was her little doll – the one she dressed up for the world to admire. And maybe, just maybe, that was how she showed the world she cared.

There was always something unspoken between us. Love, yes, but knotted with resistance, tension perhaps. She knew I'd always take my dad's side. But what she perhaps didn't realise, or maybe she did and couldn't say was – that I was just like her. Defiant. Spirited. Unapologetically curious. And maybe that's what frustrated her the most. That I was a carbon copy of her, yet I clung to him. Or maybe, just maybe, I reminded her of the version of herself she had to bury under duty, disappointment, and the heavy silence of a love gone cold.

Still, she was a character – full of fire and fizz. The life and soul of any party. She had this energy. Magnetic. Chaotic. Unforgettable. Wherever she went, laughter followed, music played louder, glasses clinked more freely. She didn't just walk into a room – she arrived. And when she arrived, the party started. Dripping in gold, bold lipstick and booming laughter. Yet behind it all was a woman holding herself together in a marriage that no longer loved her back, raising a daughter who looked far too much like freedom.

It's easy to look back in sorrow, but when I think of my parents, I try to remember the joy too – the absurdity that made them *them*. Like the time we visited my grandparents in Coventry. Mum, still on her provisional licence, insisted on driving back. Her eyesight was questionable at best, her milk bottle glasses did little to help, but Dad, ever the peacekeeper, handed her the keys. She promptly drove the wrong way round a directional bollard. Thankfully we were on the A roads. My dad erupted: *"Stop the car! Get out! You're going to kill me and my daughter. You're never driving with her in the car again!"*

Even now, I can still see it – her flailing, him fuming, me in the back seat trying not to laugh. It was chaos. Classic them. Him, all logic and restraint. Her, all mischief and momentum. Their love may have frayed at the edges, but somehow it was still stitched together with shared history and sheer force of will.

It took a long time for me to stop seeing them as just my parents, but as people too. Flawed. Hurt. Human. They had loved once. I believe that. But life had a way of eroding that love. Not all at once, but slowly – through disappointments, betrayals, grief. And still, they stayed. For us. For appearances. Because leaving just wasn't something people did back then.

Between Mum, Dad and me, there was love – tangled, imperfect, in some moments almost unbearable. But love, nonetheless. And it taught me a great deal. That love isn't always a grand gesture. Sometimes it's in the little things. A home cooked meal. A well-tied scarf. A soft glance when you're not looking. And even when it isn't what you want it to be, sometimes it's enough to know that someone stayed.

Their love for each other may have faded. But their love for me didn't. They gave what they could. My dad gave me safety. My mum gave me sparkle. Together, they gave me contrast – two sides of a coin I still carry with me. I don't romanticise their story, but I honour it. Because it shaped me. It showed me what to avoid. What to fix. When to walk. And it taught me that love, in all its messy, mismatched, misunderstood forms, is still worth writing about.

* * *

THE LESSONS I CARRY WITH ME

1. ***A child only gets one childhood:*** Its echoes last a lifetime. What we see, what we feel, and the languages we aren't given – it all shapes the love we later accept.
2. ***You can grow up in a house full of people and still feel alone:*** Presence doesn't equal connection. You can be surrounded and still feel unseen.
3. ***Sometimes the deepest truths are found in silence:*** Between two people who stopped loving each other. Watching my parents taught me that staying isn't the same as staying connected. Sometimes leaving is the kinder choice for everyone.
4. ***Love and care are not the same thing:*** Someone can love you without knowing how to love you well. Learn to unpick the difference between love that protects you – and love that controls you.
5. ***Not every lesson arrives kindly:*** Some come wrapped in sarcasm, in silence, in the sting of a raised voice or hand. But even those taught me resilience, and the grace of forgiving without forgetting.

But I finally learnt this: Parents aren't perfect, but they are powerful. My dad gave me safety; my mum gave me flair. Together, they shaped both my sparkle and my scars – parts of me I now carry, honour, and choose to heal. The love you witness becomes your template. You either recreate or rebel. I chose rebellion. I chose peace over performance, honesty over history, and leaving over losing myself.

3

THE WEIGHT OF BEING ME

I was small in size, but the expectations weighing down my shoulders were anything but. Being the eldest child often means carrying the weight of the world before you even know what it means to bear the load. You become the strong one so early, you forget softness was ever an option.

They say the firstborn is the trial run. The one parents practise on. But for me, it felt more like I was born holding a clipboard and wearing a headset. From the moment I arrived, there was a silent contract, one I never signed but was somehow bound to. I wasn't just the eldest. I was the example. The sister. The third parent. The peacekeeper. The emotional first responder to crises that were never mine.

I was not just the firstborn to my parents – I was also the firstborn daughter of all the grandchildren. One of ten. With six whole years between me and the next, my role wasn't assumed, it was inherited. As soon as she was born, so was my title. Big sister. Big energy. Big responsibility. I became a helper, a guide, a miniature matriarch in the making. No one said it out aloud. They didn't have to. It was in the glances, in the hands that passed me the baby first, in the chores quietly redirected my way.

In Asian families, there's a legacy laced into the role of the eldest. You're the glue. The keeper of calm. The one expected to hold everything and everyone together. It's not a role you choose – it's absorbed through your pores and woven into your DNA. Growing up my friends didn't always understand why I couldn't just switch off, why I was always *on*. Partners struggled with the weight I carried, the invisible load I never put down. But I'd been in training before I could even tie my own laces. Not just for myself, but for everyone else too.

My family didn't have to teach me responsibility – I lived it. My grandmother taught me how to lead with just a look. My father modelled what it meant to be dependable. My mother, with all her fire and unpredictability, showed me what it looked like to show up, even while silently falling apart. I was surrounded by strength that didn't shout, it simply got on with it.

Childhood wasn't something I stepped into. It was something I squeezed around. While my friends were out being teenagers – learning lyrics to the new boy band track, breaking curfews. I was the in-house therapist, babysitter, spokesperson, and silent negotiator. I could read tension before it even arrived, like a sailor reading a storm. While they learnt algebra, I was learning how to stick fish fingers in the oven, settle tantrums, soothe frustrations, and carry everyone else's moods like an emotional ninja.

There's no handbook for the firstborn, but there are rules – mostly unspoken. Mine were wrapped in duty. Tied with expectations, Stitched with silence. There was no space to fall apart when you were the strong one. I always had to '*know better*'. That phrase clung to me like a second skin. It didn't just mean age. It meant composure. It meant smiling when you wanted to scream. Watching others cry while you swallowed your own ache.

If I couldn't be carefree, I could at least be composed. And that became my brand. Cool. Calm. Collected. Competent. Controlled. My teachers adored me. I was the dependable student, the quiet achiever. A Prefect who knew her way around authority. My peers respected me. No one crossed the line. There was an energy I carried, even back then – a quiet '*don't mess with me*' attitude, born from the pressure of keeping everything together.

I was parenting long before I ever thought about having children. Tying shoelaces. Wiping noses. Mediating spats. Explaining things I barely understood myself. I was the buffer. The bridge. The blueprint. The one everyone counted on to get it right. Because if I didn't, who else would? My role wasn't to fall apart – it was to hold others while they did.

There were school mornings when I'd be brushing down collars; making sure shoes matched feet; homework was in bags, and someone had their inhaler. I knew everyone's routine better than they did. After school, I was back in big sister mode – listening to playground politics, packing PE kits, mediating who got the last biscuit. It wasn't heroic. It wasn't special. It was expected. It was just what I did.

Swimming lessons were their own circus act. Towels packed. Caps ready. Locker coins clutched in my hand. I remembered who hated cold water, who needed armbands, who always forgot their shampoo. While other girls my age were getting picked up from dance school, I was making sure everyone made it out of the changing rooms in one piece. I wasn't asked. I just did it. Because that's what strong girls do – they step in before anyone realises help is needed.

And yes, there was pride in being reliable. In being trusted. In being the one no one needed to worry about. But even pride becomes heavy when you carry it alone. There's a particular loneliness in the heart of a firstborn – a space where childlike wonder should live, but instead there's structure, responsibility, and expectation.

There's grief in never being allowed to unravel. I didn't even realise I was performing until I was exhausted – micromanaging my own life and everyone else's, trying to get everything just right. Not because I was a perfectionist, but because perfection felt like protection. If I did everything right, maybe nothing would break. Maybe no one would raise their voice. Maybe everyone would be okay.

I learnt to plaster a smile on my face, that if you looked closely enough, never quite reached my eyes. *"I'm fine"* became my catchphrase. Even when I wasn't.

I became a fixer in love, too. Attracting broken people like magnets. Trying to patch them up, hold them together, love them whole. I offered solutions before they could ask – because somewhere along the line, I was taught that love was something you earned by doing, not something you received by simply being.

I stayed too long in places that didn't deserve me. Not because I didn't know how to leave, but because I didn't want to let anyone down. Choosing myself felt selfish. Letting someone else crumble felt worse than crumbling myself. I didn't have boundaries, I had guilt. And guilt whispered "*Do more. Be better. Make it work.*" Until I was empty.

And then came the crash. Not dramatic, just... stillness. A kind of exhaustion that seeps into your bones. The tiredness no amount of sleep can fix. That's when I realised – I was tired of being the strong one. Tired of performing. Tired of pretending.

Healing teaches you what being the eldest never did – that you're allowed to take off the invisible cape. That being dependable doesn't mean you have to disappear. That being strong doesn't mean you can't be soft. And slowly, gently, I started to unlearn. I started to say no. I let people see the cracks. I let go of the idea that love is earned through sacrifice. Because little me – she carried so much. And she deserved to rest.

Looking back now, I see how that role shaped me. Always anticipating. Always managing. Always showing up, even when I was barely holding it together. No one ever asked what that strength was costing me. And I never offered it up. Because being the firstborn meant showing up. Every time.

At school, I played the part – the reliable one, the high-achiever, the gold star girl. But perfection came with pressure. One mistake and I'd spiral. I wasn't allowed to fail. Not when everyone was leaning on me.

At home, I was the keeper of peace. If arguments flared, I hushed the younger ones. If someone cried, I wiped their tears. If something broke, I found a way to fix it. School runs, swimming lessons, brushed hair, packed bags – I did it all, often before anyone asked. Because I thought that's what love looked like.

I became the translator between my parents and siblings – my mother's fire, my father's silence. Their words travelled through me. Softened. Filtered. Adapted, so my siblings never felt what I did.

People pleasing became my muscle memory. I didn't even realise I was saying yes before I thought about it. Agreed before I processed. And when I broke down, I didn't understand why. Until I did.

The weight of being little me with big energy is still something I'm learning to set down, piece by piece. Now, I've learnt that I don't have to carry everyone. That rest is not a reward – it's a right. That love, real love, doesn't demand depletion. It welcomes honesty. It invites boundaries. In healing, I'm learning how to be free.

* * *

THE LESSONS I CARRY WITH ME

1. ***Strength isn't about suffering in silence:*** It's about knowing when to speak and when to surrender. Real power is discerning what needs your voice – and what needs your peace. Staying quiet to keep the peace can sometimes rob you of your own.
2. ***Saying no isn't selfish, it's sacred:*** Every '*yes*' that drains you is a quiet betrayal of yourself. Protecting your energy is not just allowed – it's essential.
3. ***Dependability should never cost you your peace:*** Being the one everyone relies on is honourable, but not if it leaves you running on empty. You matter too. You always did. You always will.
4. ***Love isn't earned through effort***: It's your birthright. You don't have to over-function to be worthy. You don't have to fix to be chosen. The love given freely – without expectation – is the only kind that truly heals.
5. ***You are not responsible for everyone's happiness:*** You can love deeply and still let people carry their own burdens and emotions. Sacrificing yourself to keep others smiling only teaches them to expect your burnout.

The quiet lesson beneath it all: The little girl who held it all together still lives in me, and she too deserves to be held. She was strong when she had to be. But today, I'm giving her a rest, joy, space to breathe. Because healing isn't just letting go – it's letting her feel free.

4

THE TRIBE THAT SHAPED ME

I grew up in a family where cousins were more than relatives – they were our closest friends, our siblings in every way. The memories we created together were some of the best times in our lives. And in a world that kept shifting around us, they were the one constant. The family we chose, time and time again, even though we were born into it.

I grew up in a family where cousins weren't just cousins. They were your first friends. Your first frenemies. Your first secret keepers. We didn't need carefully curated play dates or holiday clubs. We had each other – back garden Olympics, lounge camping, dares that almost got us grounded, and storylines that only made sense to us *(some things never change)*.

We were our own universe. Self-created. Chaotic. Occasionally a bit feral.

There was a magic in those early years that you couldn't bottle even if you tried. Mismatched pyjamas. Shared toothbrushes *(don't ask).* Sleeping bags dragged into living rooms. Laughing until someone wet themselves, while getting told off because others were trying to sleep. Crying when one of us had to go home. Back then, there was no greater betrayal than a cousin going to bed without you. And no greater thrill than knowing you were getting a sleepover and a 99 Flake from the ice cream van the next day.

Being with them felt like stepping out of real life and into a world where the rules were made up on the spot and the only currency was fun. We had in-jokes and made up languages, top secret handshakes and imaginary kingdoms that we guarded with the seriousness of world leaders.

If our parents were the walls, we were the graffiti. Bright. Chaotic. Loud. Unremovable.

We didn't realise it at the time, but those bonds were teaching us about loyalty. Forgiveness. Leadership. Teamwork. How to say sorry without words. How to take the fall when someone else had the idea. How to stick together even when we were falling out. There was safety in our chaos – a sense that, no matter what else was happening in the world, if you had your cousins, you were good.

They were my practice people. My soft landings. My partners in punishment. We learnt love, trust, and alliance before we even knew what those were things. And while we grew up, some of us drifted, found our own people in the world, there's a corner of my heart that still belongs to them. The part that knows all the words to our secret songs. That remembers exactly who cheated at Monopoly. That still laughs at jokes we haven't told in decades.

Because cousins are forever friends. Born into your bloodline, bonded by your childhood. And no matter how far life takes you from each other, you never forget the ones who knew you before you even knew yourself.

There's twelve years between me and my brother, but I never felt like an only child – not really. Not when I was surrounded by cousins. Loud. Loyal. Wildly inappropriate cousins who filled every silence before it had the chance to become lonely.

On my dad's side, we were like a four-piece band. Three boys and me. Our very own Famous Four – minus the cat, double the mischief. We all lived within walking distance, and though I was third in the pecking order, I was undoubtedly the ringleader. The brains behind every plan. The mouth behind every excuse. The spark behind most of the trouble. I had a talent for coming up with the most ludicrous ideas, and an even better talent for convincing others to follow through with them.

I still remember the day I tried to get on a bus with my older cousin. I was four. He was six. That should've been enough of a red flag for any responsible adult, but I had confidence for days. I'd somehow managed to charm the bus driver into believing that, yes, of course our parents knew we were going. In fact, they told us to go. I even had the bus fare ready, which only added to the illusion.

He was just about to shut the doors when, like something out of a soap opera, my mum came charging across the street. Hair flying. Eyes blazing. Screaming at the poor man: *"Are you stupid or something, letting two children on a bus alone? What's wrong with you?"* Meanwhile, I stood there, wide eyed and innocent, watching him get the telling off of his life while quietly slipping my change back into my pocket.

Mum's side of the family? Now that was a bit more complicated – for them, anyway. For me, it was simple. I got on like a house on fire with my mum's sisters' grandkids. We were thick as thieves, and just as destructive. But her brother's side? Not so much. They were too stiff for my liking *(thankfully they mellowed as adults)*. All rules and righteousness. I was allergic to anything too strait laced, even then. I preferred the wild side. I was the wild side.

When my three cousins came over, with their perfect plaits, the fun really began. We'd run up to Mum and Dad's bedroom, lock the door, draw the curtains, and turn into secret spies. Across the road was a large public toilet, and not the usual kind. The sort that attracted all sorts of shady characters. The ones who went in and didn't come out for ages.

Naturally, our imaginations ran wild. We'd press our faces to the window and make up the most elaborate stories about what went on down those mysterious steps. Secret spies. Secret potions. People changing identities. Nothing was off the table. That window became our theatre, and those characters, our cast. I think that's where my love of people watching began. I was always too curious for my own good. Still am.

We had no idea then how golden those moments were – locked away in a stuffy bedroom with sticky hands, stale crisps, and imaginations that could power a thousand Netflix shows. That was our little world, full of storytelling, giggles we tried to muffle with pillows, and theories so wild we convinced ourselves they had to be true.

We weren't just bored kids. We were investigative journalists. Undercover agents. Directors of our own low budget spy thriller. The budget? Two pens, a notepad, and a pair of binoculars I once won in a school raffle.

Those days weren't about doing anything particularly grand. They were about just being. Being together. Being curious. Being kids without the pressure of being perfect. No curated childhoods or parenting manuals. Just unfiltered, chaotic joy with people who didn't judge your spelling mistakes, your silly jokes, or the hairstyle you created on your Girls World doll.

And when we weren't watching the world from the upstairs window, we were creating our own dramas downstairs. Singing into hairbrushes; inventing dance routines; turning pillow-cases into saris and strutting down imaginary runways like we owned Milan. Every visit turned into an event. A performance. An unspoken competition seeing who could be the loudest, the cheekiest, or the most dramatic (*spoiler alert: it was usually me*).

But even the chaos had a kind of comfort. We might have been loud, messy, and occasionally at war over who got the last choc ice or raspberry ripple ice cream tub – but our bond was built on something real. Something deeper than just blood.

It was the kind of love that didn't need daily maintenance. The kind that could lie dormant for months and then reignite the second someone walked through the front door with a bag of pick 'n' mix and a story to tell.

Sometimes I wonder if the grown-ups knew how much we leant on each other. How, when things got tense downstairs – voices rising, doors slamming, silences stretching too long, we'd retreat to the safety of cousinhood. We'd distract each other with dares and dances and daft games. We'd create noise to drown out the things we didn't understand.

Without realising it, we were building resilience. Learning how to show up for each other in small ways, long before any of us could put that into words.

They were my first audience. My first supporters. My first soft place to land. I learned how to laugh at myself because of them, and how to stand up for myself because of them. They challenged me. Protected me. Took the blame for me. Snitched on me, sure – but never in a way that really hurt. Because cousins aren't just witnesses to your childhood, they're co-conspirators, co-authors.

We've all grown up now. Moved. Changed. Started our own families. Some of us are still thick as thieves. Others drifted with time and distance. But the imprint remains. I still see pieces of them in who I am. In the way I tell stories. In how I navigate conflict. Even in the way I laugh so hard I cry.

My cousins were my first tribe. They taught me how to belong,

long before I ever learned to stand on my own two feet. And no matter where life takes us, a part of me will always be that little girl at the window – eyes wide, ideas wild, surrounded by the safest kind of chaos.

* * *

THE LESSONS I CARRY WITH ME

1. ***Childhood friendships don't need planning:*** They just need proximity. Cousins were proof that shared space builds shared souls. We didn't need reasons to be together – just the chance to be.
2. ***Imagination is the beginning of identity:*** Those games, those dares, those made up stories weren't silly. They were a rehearsal for who we'd become.
3. ***You don't need the same personalities to belong to the same tribe:*** My cousins were nothing like me – yet exactly like me in all the ways that counted.
4. ***Laughter is the language of connection:*** The in-jokes, the giggle fits, the laugh crying over nonsense – that was how we built intimacy.
5. ***Cousins are the only friends who know your truth and love you anyway:*** They saw the tantrums, the weird phases, the home haircut disasters – and they still chose you.

Here's what stayed with me: The girl before me wasn't lost, she was learning. Watching. Imagining. Leading. Loving. That window. Those stories. Those moments of spying weren't nosiness – they were the start of a storyteller. She didn't need polish. She needed space. And in those messy, magical cousin filled days, she got it.

II

THE GIRLS BEFORE ME

Before I knew who I was, I learned who I needed to be. Polished. Prepared. Impossible to hurt.

There were versions of me no one ever really met. The quiet one. The clever one. The one who always had it together, even when she didn't. So I built armour out of smiles, silence, quick wit, and always being 'fine.' Soft for some. Sharp for others. But never fully seen. Never enough to be truly known. And yet... even then, something in me was watching. Waiting. Taking notes. Those girls weren't fake – they were just unfinished, protecting what hadn't healed yet.

This was my middle. The mask. The armour. The girls I'd been – before me.

5

THE EARLY ECHOES OF ME

Before we become ourselves, we perform ourselves. We shape-shift. We shrink. We smile when we want to speak. And sometimes, we try so hard to fit in, we forget we were never meant to blend – we were meant to become. There's a version of you that comes before the confidence. She isn't wrong. She isn't weak. She's just early. I didn't see it then, but she was my beginning. The girl I needed to be before I became the woman I am today.

Before I learned to walk in heels, I was still tripping over who I thought I had to be.

There was a version of me, in my school years, who existed before confidence arrived. She was polite, agreeable. Always slightly apologising for taking up space. She laughed a little too loudly to fill awkward silences and wore clothes that didn't quite match her mood.

She wasn't fake – she was just... unfinished.

And the truth is, we all have a '*before*' version of ourselves. The girl we shaped to fit into spaces that were never meant for us. I loved her. I just didn't realise she wasn't the final draft.

At school, I was never the loud one. Never the front row hand-raiser. But I wasn't invisible either. There was a quiet confidence about me, a stillness that said '*don't mess with me*'. I didn't need to shout to be heard. My silence had its own kind of authority. You could see it in the way I walked down the corridor – head held high, eyes forward. Not because I was full of myself, but because I knew exactly how far people could push me before I pushed back. I had an invisible line, and everyone knew not to cross it.

That confidence, though? It wasn't all mine. I was protected by a crew – cousins in the years above me. Scary. Loud. Legendary. The mere mention of their names made trouble walk the other way. If I had a problem, they handled it before I even knew it was mine to handle.

No one dared say a word to me unless they wanted to answer to them. That kind of protection gave me space to breathe. I didn't need to puff out my chest or raise my voice. I had quiet power – the kind that comes when you know someone's got your back.

I was never boy-obsessed. Not like some of the girls around me. While they scribbled initials in notebooks and swooned at the sight of floppy fringes and fake bravado, I was just trying to get through the day with my head down and my reputation intact. I didn't even notice when a boy noticed me. I wasn't interested in being picked or praised. I wanted peace. Predictability. To move through the hours without incident. I wasn't shy. I just didn't see the point in making noise for the sake of it. And if a boy did try to speak to me, I'd blink in confusion – half annoyed they were interrupting whatever story I was writing in my head.

There were things I loved, though – English, maths, sports. English was my escape route. The way words could become armour and stories could become shelter. I loved how writing let me say what I didn't know how to say out loud. I lost myself in poetry, pieced myself together in prose. I could vanish into a book and re-emerge calmer. Braver. More whole. It was the one place I didn't have to perform; I could just be a girl with a pencil, rewriting her own narrative.

I remember winning a creative writing competition once. Nothing major, just something small at school. But it made me feel like I mattered. Like my voice, on paper at least, had power. I didn't shout in real life, but I roared in essays. Words gave me the permission I hadn't yet given myself. I wasn't popular, but my work was pinned to the wall. That meant something. Sometimes when the teacher read my work aloud, I'd sit there pretending to be nonchalant, but inside I was buzzing. That was my applause. That was my proof.

And sports? That was where I came alive. I was a force to be reckoned with on the netball court – team captain and centre forward. I had the meanest serve in tennis *(my secret weapon)*. And hockey? Well, let's just say if a girl clipped my ankle with her stick, I'd return the favour. Perfectly timed and with enough force to make her think twice next time.

I wasn't a troublemaker, but I wasn't soft either. On the field, I had bite. I could charm a referee with a look, lead a team with conviction, and still keep my knee-high socks spotless.

That was my magic.

I liked structure. Rules. Purpose. The feeling of being part of a team. And maybe that's why I loved it – because on those courts and pitches, I didn't have to question where I belonged. I just played. I led. I scored. And when I walked off, sweat on my brow and fire in my chest, I felt seen.

But the one thing I hated? Getting dirty.

Cross country? No thanks. Rolling in mud or sitting on grass without a blanket underneath me? Absolutely not. I could command a team, break into a sprint, or chase down a ball with fierce determination – but mud near my knees or dirt on my socks? That was where I drew the line. Even on the pitch, there was always a little part of me that refused to compromise my standards. Neat and composed. Always.

I was obsessed with neatness. My planner was colour-coded, my pencil case pristine, my homework completed with time to spare. That was how I stayed in control. In a world that often felt unpredictable, organisation was my armour. It gave me structure. It gave me safety. I could sit in the chaos of a lunchroom but still feel anchored because my folders were in order. Even my packed lunches were organised – sandwich first, crisps second, chocolate third, and fruit if I had time.

Even back then I kept my circle small – a few close friends, the kind of girls who shared their crisps and their secrets. We weren't the cool crowd, nor were we the misfits. We were the in-betweeners. Good girls with just enough mischief to be interesting.

We talked too much in lessons, laughed too loudly at lunch, and imagined futures so far away they didn't need to make sense. We passed notes in class, rating teachers out of ten for likeability, and choreographed dance routines to Madonna's hits during sleepovers.

Some days those friendships were everything. Other days, they were... complicated.

I was loyal to a fault – the kind of girl who'd lend you her last pencil but not her patience if you crossed her. I knew how to hold a grudge without ever saying a word. If you hurt me, I wouldn't scream about it, I'd just stop showing up. Quiet cuts, the kind you don't see coming.

Looking back, I wonder if I was learning boundaries, or just afraid of confrontation? Maybe a little of both.

And despite how '*together*' I seemed, there were days I came home and collapsed face-first onto my bed. Not because I was tired from schoolwork, but from the performance. From the smiling. The negotiating. The blending. Being liked for a version of me that wasn't quite true was its own kind of exhaustion. But still, I kept going. Because that's what girls like me did.

I think I was always watching back then. Observing. Listening. Figuring people out. I'd clock the smallest changes – a new pencil case, a different tone of voice, the way someone's smile didn't quite reach their eyes that day. I was curious, cautious even. The kind of girl who could read a room better than she could read a map *(some things never change).* I noticed everything. Even when I said nothing. And when I did speak, it was measured. Deliberate, like I knew every word had weight.

Sometimes I wonder what teachers thought of me. The neat girl. The quiet one. The one who never caused a fuss but never faded either. I didn't get in trouble. I didn't seek attention. I just... existed neatly between the lines, until I was ready to draw my own.

Looking back, I can see her now – the girl I used to be. All shoulders and second guesses. Soft eyes and scribbled dreams.

She didn't know she was growing into someone strong.
She didn't realise her silence was a kind of strength.
She was just doing her best to make it through the day without cracking.
She wasn't broken.
She wasn't behind.
She was just early.

And looking back, I'm proud of her.

* * *

THE LESSONS I CARRY WITH ME

1. ***Strength doesn't always arrive with a roar:*** Power doesn't always come in decibels. Sometimes it walks quietly, head held high. It's not always about fighting back – sometimes it's about knowing where your line is and holding it without explanation.
2. ***Not chasing what everyone else wants is its own kind of peace:*** I wasn't disinterested in boys; I was uninterested in performing for attention. That wasn't rebellion – that was self-respect.
3. ***Quiet is not the same as passive:*** I wasn't voiceless. I was intentional. I knew when to speak, and more importantly, when not to waste my words.
4. ***Even the early versions of you are whole:*** The girl who second guessed herself, who measured every move – she wasn't broken. She was just building.
5. ***School isn't just about education:*** It's training for life. Every group project, every skipped heartbeat before speaking up – it was all practice for becoming someone who could lead.

And maybe the greatest lesson was this: I wasn't lost. I didn't need fixing. I needed witnessing. And I see that girl now – not as someone I outgrew, but as someone who helped me become. She still lives in me. But now, I'm letting her be fully seen.

6

THE GIRL THEY DIDN'T SEE WAS ME

I wasn't invisible, I was overlooked. Misread. Boxed in. But people made up their minds about me long before I opened my mouth. I wasn't the loudest. I wasn't the prettiest. But I was the one they'd remember – not because I fought to be seen, but because I quietly became someone worth seeing. I didn't need the spotlight to prove my worth. My presence arrived long before my words did. And in rooms that had already decided who I was, I stayed silent. Not out of shyness, but out of knowing. Because sometimes, it's the girl who watches, who waits, who listens, who ends up becoming the one they should have paid attention to. That presence, that quiet strength, that unspoken power... that's something I will carry with me. Always.

College. The great in-between. It didn't come with sweeping declarations or the grand reinventions they sell you in the movies. It came quietly. Like a side street you turn into without even noticing, but one that eventually leads you somewhere meaningful.

I wasn't the girl anyone expected much from. Not because I lacked ability, far from it, but because I didn't fit the expected mould. I wasn't skinny. I wasn't effortlessly pretty. I didn't giggle on cue or play dumb to be liked. I didn't scream confidence, but I wasn't weak either. I flew under the radar – not quite invisible, but always a little out of focus.

At first, I had Keira – my lunchtime partner-in-crime, my unspoken ally, my ride-or-die. Tall. Lean. Curly hair. Flawless skin, and a laugh that made boys think they had a chance *(they didn't)*. We were a duo no one expected. She was the hot one. I was the teammate. But together, we were unstoppable.

Our weapon of choice? Table football. Most days, you'd find us there, in the common room, dominating the game like we were defending a title. Left hand. Right hand. Silent eye contact and strategy. We didn't just play, we annihilated. The boys circled the table every break, pretending it was about the game. But deep down, I always wondered – were they shocked that two girls were this good at something so typically *'theirs' or* were they just watching Keira while I lined up the winning shots?

Either way, it didn't matter. Because in those moments, when I was spinning rods and slamming in goals with Keira laughing beside me, I wasn't the girl in the background. I wasn't the one trying to be seen. I was the one winning. That table gave me something no mirror ever could – a sense of presence. A moment of being undeniably there.

The boys, they hated it. Not all, but enough. They weren't used to being outplayed, especially not by two girls who didn't flinch under pressure. We didn't trash talk, we didn't need to, the scoreboard did it for us. That quiet confidence. That refusal to apologise for being brilliant at something they claimed ownership of – it rattled them.

Then Keira left. Halfway through the year, life pulled her elsewhere, and just like that, I was flying solo. Keira-less in a world that suddenly felt three sizes too big. So, I did what any girl on the brink of reinvention would do – I found a new tribe.

We were like Enid Blyton's Famous Five, except we swapped jam sandwiches for Rimmel eyeliner and a spritz of Bodyshop's Dewberry scent.

There was Maria: Tall. Gorgeous, and the kind of girl who floated through a room like she owned the air in it. She wasn't loud, but people noticed when she entered. Every boy wanted to date her, and every girl wanted to be her friend – or at least be near enough to catch some of her glow. She had that effortless kind of allure, like she didn't have to try and somehow still won the room.

Eva: A little pocket rocket in her trademark cycling shorts and Timberlands, with a smile that could stop traffic. She didn't just enter a room, she charged into it like she owned the place. College wasn't her path, but her stories – equal parts EastEnders and epic, became daily common room chatter.

Becca: Chaos personified. All limbs, loud thoughts, and coffee spills. She was lovable even when she tripped over air and apologised to furniture.

Hannah: The kind of girl who could make even a black bin liner look cool. She never followed trends – she was the trend. Effortlessly stylish. Aloof in a way that made you want to impress her. She had an eye for the extraordinary in the ordinary. Made jeans look couture, scarves iconic, and always seemed three seasons ahead of everyone else.

And then there was me. I floated somewhere in the middle. The girl with the great hair, good skin, and just enough eyeliner to pass as put-together. I didn't try to turn heads, I just didn't want to trip over them. Not popular, not invisible. I got on better with boys. They were easier – less drama, less decoding.

The popular girls didn't like me. Not because I was loud or tried to compete – in fact, it was quite the opposite. I didn't play their games, I didn't need their approval, and that made me... inconvenient. I was the girl who didn't beg for a seat at their table, and somehow, that turned me into a threat.

Then David appeared. He didn't go to our college but hung around enough that we all knew him. Tall. Broad. Stupidly good-looking. The kind of boy who made even the popular girls forget they were supposed to act indifferent. And just like that, the invisible tension turned into outright disdain. Suddenly, I wasn't just the quiet one they could dismiss – I was the quiet one who'd '*won*' something they wanted. Or at the very least, something they felt entitled to.

Their glances became sharper, the silence heavier. They didn't say anything cruel to my face – that would have required courage. But I felt it in the way conversations would stop when

I entered a room. In the sideways looks. In the way they never spoke to me, but always noticed me. David never understood it. He'd laugh it off, *"You're imagining it."* But I wasn't. Girls like that don't need to speak their dislike out loud. They just exhale it in your direction and hope it chokes you.

And while girls whispered, some boys sneered. Not the ones who liked me – the ones who didn't understand me. Like Shaylen. He decided, for reasons unbeknown, that I thought I was better than him. One day, in the middle of a normal afternoon, he grabbed my hand and said, *"Look at your palms, they're so fat. Now look at mine."* It wasn't the words that he used. It was the way he weaponised them. Casual cruelty. Aimed to diminish.

I didn't flinch. I didn't cry. I just pulled my hand away and said *"fuck you."* He didn't get to define me. But of course, it stayed with me. Words like that do. Especially when you're still shaping who you are.

Still, I had moments. Little flashes where I mattered. I'd make someone laugh – really laugh. Say something sharp, observant, just enough cheek to crack through the tension. Suddenly, my voice was heard.

College taught me that not every friendship is built on mutual admiration. Sometimes, people don't like you because you hold a mirror up to something in them that they're not ready to face. I realised early on that some girls found me threatening without me doing a single thing. Just existing was enough.

I gravitated toward the boys – not because I needed attention, but because with them, there was no competition. No back-handed compliments. They laughed at my jokes, admired my wit, respected my space, and saw me as someone they could be real with. And in that space, I not only grew, I flourished.

But make no mistake, that didn't mean I didn't feel the sting. The sting of being misjudged. Of walking into a room and sensing the whispers. Of knowing I was being spoken about in hushed tones. And still, I stayed grounded. Because deep down, I knew I wasn't made for popularity – I was made for purpose.

There were days I wanted to cry in frustration at the injustice of it all. But never in front of others. I was raised to stay composed. I'd put my music on, straighten up and just walk away. That was my rebellion. My quiet proof that I was still standing.

Funny thing is, decades later, the same people that exhibited so much hate in college reached out to me. Shaylen tracked me down to apologise for his appalling behaviour. I forgave him – not because he deserved it, but because I didn't want his hurtful words to haunt me forever. Even some of those same girls circled back, with praise, with recognition, with "*I always knew you would...*"

Maybe they did. Or maybe I just became the girl they didn't realise was me all along. Because while they played their parts, I was still writing mine. And I didn't need a spotlight to know I was becoming someone worth seeing.

* * *

THE LESSONS I CARRY WITH ME

1. ***You don't need the spotlight to be unforgettable:*** Power doesn't always perform. Sometimes it just walks in, unbothered, and dares the room to catch up.
2. ***Being misunderstood is not your cue to explain:*** Let them misread you. The people who matter will take the time to see you properly. Their discomfort is not your responsibility. You weren't made to be manageable.
3. ***Real friendship doesn't audition you:*** It welcomes you as you are. No edits. No performance. No shrink-to-fit instructions.
4. ***Quiet confidence is disruptive:*** Nothing unsettles people more than a woman who doesn't flinch, doesn't chase, and doesn't need to be liked.
5. ***Forgiveness is closure for yourself:*** I didn't release the other person from their guilt, because they earned it. I released them because I deserved peace.

But here's the thing: I thought I had to become someone else to be seen. I didn't. I just had to stop dimming the girl who was there all along. The one who never needed permission to take up space. The one who let them whisper, let them watch – and kept walking anyway. I learned that presence doesn't beg. It simply is. And in the end, the girl they overlooked became the woman they couldn't ignore.

7

THE ARMOUR I CALLED ME

Sometimes the strongest girls wear the heaviest armour – not because they want to fight, but because they've had to. There's a certain kind of girl who walks into a room like she's untouchable – not because she thinks she is, but because life taught her she had to be. She's all bite and brilliance, wrapped in sarcasm and perfectly timed exits. You call her difficult. She calls it survival. I call her me.

University was never about self-discovery for me – it was about self defence. A continuation, not a reinvention. I didn't arrive hoping to find myself. I arrived knowing exactly who I wasn't willing to be anymore.

By the time I stepped onto campus, the little softness I'd once possessed had been scorched off me. What remained was armour. Not the shiny kind you show off, but the invisible kind. The kind that hardens your tone. Sharpens your wit. Makes your silence speak louder than your words.

I didn't come alone. Eva quit her job and came with me. I enrolled officially; she faked being a student so well you'd have thought she ran the place. Together we were chaos and calm, chalk and cheese. I was five foot five, with pale skin, a short silky bob, and eyes that confused people of my ethnicity. Eva was four foot nothing with curls for days, deep brown skin, and a smile that could stop traffic mid-flow.

Style-wise, we were opposites too. I was all clean lines and fitted trousers – my signature cream ones earned me the nickname *'Skipants Suki'*. Eva wore cycling shorts like it was a lifestyle. She showed skin, I showed restraint. But together? We worked. She was my ride or die.

We moved in with Maria and Becca, who were already a year deep into uni life. Maria let us share the box room in her rented house. From day one, I had the lowdown on who to avoid. The charmers. The liars. The heartbreakers in designer belts. So when I walked into the student union, straight to the pool table like it had my name on it, I already had the playbook.

That's when I saw him – Jags. Handsome. Polished. Magnetic. Surrounded by women, of course. We locked eyes. He smiled. I nodded. Cue Maria, sliding in like a stage whisper *"I told you to stay away from him. He's bad news."* So I looked away. But let's be honest – bad news has a funny way of pulling focus.

I'd sharpened by then. Sarcasm was my native tongue. Humour was a blade. Red lipstick, my war paint. I was quick. Sharp. Always ten seconds ahead of whatever line someone thought they could use on me. Jags tried. Oh, he tried. But I ran rings around men like him. I'd allow them to flirt with me, but unless you had substance, you weren't touching a thing.

Every night out threw a new contender into the ring. Boys who thought they could charm their way in, only to back off under the weight of my unbothered stare and verbal side-eye. Then came the one I didn't see coming... Tariq.

He walked past. Then backtracked. Looked me up and down. Smiled. Cue, my perfectly tweezed, raised eyebrow. *"Can I help you with something?"*

"No thanks," he smirked. *"I'm just admiring."* And walked off.

Half an hour later, I saw him again, standing alone. So I returned the favour. Slowly eyeing him up, top to bottom, I paused. *"Can I help you with something?"* He smirked.

"No thanks," I said. *"Just admiring."* pivoting on my well heeled shoes, I vanished.

That was the beginning of three and a half years in one of the most toxic relationships I've ever encountered. But that's enough about Tariq for now. You can meet him a little later.

Something shifted in me that day. I realised I wasn't invisible anymore. I wasn't flying under the radar. The wallflower had bloomed – and she was standing centre stage. I was getting male attention, lots of it. And for a moment, I thought maybe I'd arrived. That maybe being wanted was a kind of winning *(spoiler alert: it wasn't).*

Because I wasn't prepared to entertain a weak man. Not really. But I still hadn't unlearned the belief that love meant fixing someone. That if I could just hold the chaos together, it might eventually feel like peace. Underneath the sharpness, I was still the girl who'd once sat quietly in classrooms, silently watching, waiting. But now I had volume. I had presence. I had posture. I wore my hair like a crown and my confidence like a warning.

They called me hard. Cold. Intimidating. I called it boundaries.

But that armour didn't come out of nowhere. It was forged long before I ever stepped onto campus. I grew up watching a version of love that came wrapped in tension, silence, and sharp edges. Love wasn't soft. It was conditional. Uneven. Performed more than it was felt. And somewhere in that environment, I learned that closeness wasn't safe, and vulnerability came with consequences.

So I built walls. High ones. Decorated in charisma. Reinforced with wit. Disguised with independence. I became fluent in letting people close without ever letting them in. Because softness, to me, looked like weakness. And weakness got you hurt.

Girls who cried in bathrooms? The ones who wore their hearts on their sleeves? I watched them get broken. Ghosted. Humiliated. I couldn't be that girl. I wouldn't be that girl. So I became the girl who saw the heartbreak before it happened. Who walked out before she could be walked over. Who made you laugh, made you wonder, but never let you close enough to see the cracks.

That kind of strength? It makes you feel like nothing can touch you. Until one day, you realise... it also means nothing can really reach you. Because building walls doesn't just keep heartbreak out – it keeps connection out too. And you don't notice it at first. You're too busy basking in your own independence, mistaking solitude for strength. You convince yourself you don't need anyone, because needing has never ended well. You take pride in being low maintenance. Unreadable. Hard to impress. You sit at the centre of your own fortress, admiring how few people have made it past the gates.

But late at night, when the noise dies down and the bravado quiets, it creeps in – the ache. The emptiness of never being truly held, because you never let anyone close enough to try. The loneliness of always being the strong one. The exhausting loop of pretending you're fine when really, you're just well-practised in not falling apart.

There's a silence in being guarded that no one talks about. A kind of grief for all the moments you didn't let yourself feel, all the people you pushed away before they had a chance to prove you wrong. You wear your armour so well, you forget it's even there. Until one day, someone touches your shoulder gently, and you flinch. Not because it hurts, but because kindness feels foreign.

You realise then that strength is only part of the story. That maybe true courage is letting yourself be seen without the layers. That the bravest thing you can do is not fight, but allow softness to coexist with your strength. That letting someone in isn't weak. It's human.

And slowly, you begin to loosen the buckle. Not all at once. Not for everyone. But just enough to breathe. Just enough to remind yourself that being open doesn't mean being exposed. That boundaries can protect – but they can also imprison if you never open the gate.

It's a strange kind of power, learning to put the armour down. But the girl beneath it? She was never less. She was just waiting to feel safe enough to step out. And once she does, she's still you. Just softer. Just braver. Just ready.

And yet, the thing about armour is... it's heavy. And after a while, you forget you're wearing it. University made me fierce. But it also showed me that real power isn't always in the sharp edges – sometimes it's in knowing when to soften. Because even the girl who didn't take any shit... still just wanted to be seen.

She was still me.

* * *

THE LESSONS I CARRY WITH ME

1. ***Not everyone who admires you, will honour you:*** Attention isn't the same as affection. Wanting you is not the same as choosing you. Desire is loud. Respect is quiet but consistent. Learn the difference.
2. ***Some armour looks like red lips and sarcasm:*** The heaviest kind hides in silence, invisible to the naked eye. The kind that smiles while scanning for danger. That walks into a room already bracing.
3. ***Boundaries are a love language:*** They're not walls to keep love out, but gates you control. You decide who gets close, and how far they're allowed in.
4. ***They'll call you difficult when they can't control you:*** Let them. That label isn't a flaw. It's proof you stopped shrinking to be liked.
5. ***You can be fierce and still crave softness:*** Wanting to be seen, truly seen, doesn't make you weak. It makes you ready.

And one more truth: I wore the armour because it felt safer than softness. But armour is lonely. It keeps the world out. It keeps you in. I waited too long to put it down. But I'm here now. Not walking into rooms untouched. Just learning to walk in without the need to be untouchable.

8

THE GIRL WHO PLAYED ME

I was born wearing what looked like confidence. Shoulders back. Head held high. A voice that didn't flinch. But the truth? I was just a really good actress. There's a version of me that believed success was a costume – sharp blazer, polished voice, a to-do list that never ended. I wore it well. Too well. So well, no one noticed I was terrified of being found out. I smiled while panicking. I showed up while doubting. I performed while falling apart. That girl didn't fail. But she did lose herself trying not to.

There's a particular kind of exhaustion that comes from pretending to have your shit together. Not the kind where you're actually managing life well – just the kind where you look like you are.

Hair brushed. Blazer sharp. Smile rehearsed. Voice steady. You arrive on time. You make eye contact. You nod like you understand the plethora of terms they're using, when really, you're just praying no one asks a follow-up question.

Welcome to the working world – where confidence is currency and imposter syndrome wears heels.

I didn't walk into my first real job feeling ready. I walked in with a carefully curated mask and the quiet panic of someone waiting to be found out. I wasn't underqualified. I was underprepared. Underwhelmed. Under the illusion that everyone else had it figured out except me. But here's the truth no one tells you – we all start off pretending.

When I look at how my parents and grandparents worked, it's clear, Asians are pre-programmed with a '*work hard*' mentality. Failure is not an option. And they don't understand work-life balance. They don't rest, they graft. Happily working twice as hard for half the reward, because effort is its own currency. And I grew up watching that. So of course, I followed suit.

I sort of fell into my work life. Finished uni. Moved back home. Took a temp role in a marketing department and absolutely loved it. But being back at home felt suffocating. The freedom I'd tasted at uni now felt like a dream I was being forced to wake up from. So I did what any self-respecting, semi-broke, freedom-chasing twenty-something would do – I packed my bags and headed back to London.

I landed a job in one of the capital's top marketing agencies. But not in marketing. No. I was a PA. That's what three years and a degree in Psychology and Sociology got me. A diary and a landline. Still, I said yes. Because I had bills, ambition, and a point to prove.

I got on well with my boss. Eventually, I confessed that I'd taken the PA role just to get my foot into marketing. She didn't bat an eyelid. She always knew. I was built for more. She said I could join the marketing team, as long as I kept doing my PA role too *(on the same wage)*. And I said yes. Of course I did. Because women like me were taught to say yes and prove our worth in the doing. Every payday, I'd check my bank balance and laugh. £11,000 starting salary. In one of the most expensive cities in the world. But I didn't care. I was in. I was learning. I was faking it. And I was loving it.

Eventually I left. Freelanced a bit. And then came the moment – the one I'll never forget. The one that changed my life forever.

I walked into one of the biggest, most renowned agencies in London. The job? Account Manager for a great confectionery brand. But sitting across from me was what can only be described as a posh school ma'am – complete with pearls and posture that could cut glass. Now, I'm not the kind of girl who's easily intimidated, but that day, I was rattled. That interview was horrific. I knew, before I'd even buttoned up my coat, that I hadn't got the job. I was right.

Three months later, I got a freelance gig at a retail agency – in the same building as the Cadbury interview. I was thriving. Until one day, my boss rang. *"Suki, we've had a pitch come in for a large dairy brand. Our sister agency has a conflict of interest, so can't officially pitch. You're the only one with the right experience. Would you like to work on it?"*

Hell yes I did.

I walked into the room. And guess who's there? The school ma'am. Turns out she was running the pitch. You couldn't make this stuff up if you tried. Life always loves a dramatic full circle. We spent two weeks on that pitch. When we wrapped up, she called me into her office. "*Suki,*" she said, "*you are one of the best Account Managers I've ever worked with. If we win the pitch, would you come and work for me, as a Senior Account Manager?*"

Oh, the irony. I looked her dead in the face and said, "*You don't remember me, do you?*"

She stared back. "*Since the minute you walked into that room, I've been trying to place you. But I just can't.*"

So I told her. "*Three months ago, you interviewed me. For a role on the Cadbury account, as an Account Manager. You didn't think I was good enough. And now here we are – you, perched on your chair, telling me I'm one of the best, offering me a role above the one I initially applied for. Funny how life works.*"

She wasn't used to being challenged. I could see it in her eyes. She was used to being the sharpest in the room. But I wasn't raised to be weak. Even back then, I had bigger kahunas than most men. She retorted. "*Maybe you're not good at interviewing, Suki. You should work on that.*"

I smiled, calmly. "*Or maybe you need to look at your interview technique. You made a girl who isn't naturally nervous so nervous she failed. Imagine how many other great candidates you've missed out on for the same reason. Maybe I'm not the issue here.*"

Surprisingly, she laughed. She respected my honesty and my challenge. *"Welcome to the team, Suki."*

That was the start of it all. The start of my real career and a beautiful friendship. The climb. The evolution. The version of me that walked into boardrooms like I owned them, even if inside I was still that temp wondering if she belonged.

From there, I rose. Fast. Promotions came quicker than my tax code could catch up. And every single time, I questioned if I deserved it. Did I really know what I was doing or was I just really good at acting like I did?

Fear became my motivator. Not the loud, dramatic kind. The quiet, gnawing kind that whispers at the back of your mind, *"you're going to get found out."* That this time, this meeting, this pitch, this email, you'll slip. You'll stutter. You'll say the wrong thing. You'll be exposed.

So, I doubled down. I stayed back later. Checked things twice. Three times. Rehearsed lines in my head before calls and meetings. Took on more. Said yes to things I wasn't ready for, because saying no felt like an admission of inadequacy. The irony? I was excelling. Clients loved me. My team relied on me. But the more I succeeded, the more I feared I'd fail. I couldn't let up. Because if I did, maybe they'd realise I didn't belong here after all.

The truth is, when you grow up trying to be the glue that holds everything together, good enough doesn't feel like a destination. It feels like a moving target. You can get all the praise in the world, but if you don't believe it, it slides right off – like you're Teflon-coated in doubt.

I wore my competence like armour. I was always in control, even when I felt like I was about to unravel. Smiling on the outside, to-do list-sure, while my inner voice was whispering, '*they're going to realise you're winging it.*' But I had a superpower too – fear. It didn't paralyse me. It propelled me.

Because there are two kinds of people in this world – those who run at the first sign of fear. And those who feel it, taste it, swallow it, and keep moving anyway.

I learnt fear was my kryptonite. But I also learnt it could be my superpower. Not because it felt good. But because it forced me to grow. To push. To climb. To show up when I wanted to disappear. And the more I pushed, the more I realised – I was good. Really good. Just not always good at believing it.

There were promotions I turned down because I didn't feel worthy – but got anyway. Not because I was lucky. Because I was ready, even when I didn't feel like I was.

I know now that self-doubt doesn't disappear with success. It shapeshifts. It waits. Even now, 25 years in, I still have moments. The voice that says – "*You don't know what you're doing. They're going to see right through you.*" But the difference now? I know how to answer back.

I remind myself of what I've built. Of the times I walked into rooms I wasn't invited to and left them better. Of the girl who said yes when she was terrified, who made fear her fuel, and wore her competence like war paint.

Because yes, I still get scared. But now I know – I'm not scared because I'm not enough. I'm scared because I am. Because I care. Because I'm still becoming.

* * *

THE LESSONS I CARRY WITH ME

1. ***Imposter syndrome lies in your own voice:*** The doubt that whispers *"you're not enough"* sounds like you, but it isn't. Learn to question it. Learn to answer back.
2. ***You can be excellent and still uncertain:*** High performance doesn't cancel out self-doubt. You can be thriving on paper and still only surviving inside. They can coexist.
3. ***Confidence can be a costume:*** Just because someone looks like they have it all together doesn't mean they do. We're all winging it. Some just have better tailoring.
4. ***Praise won't save you if you don't believe it:*** You can get all the validation in the world, but if you don't value yourself, it bounces right off. Healing starts on the inside.
5. ***The rooms that reject you aren't your ceiling:*** Just because one person couldn't see your magic doesn't mean it wasn't there. Sometimes, rejection is just redirection with better lighting.

And one more truth: I thought working harder would make the doubts go away. It didn't. I rose anyway. I won anyway. I stayed in the room anyway. The voice still comes sometimes. But now I know what it is. And I know who I am. I know how to answer back. *"I belong here. I always did."*

9

THE BALANCE THAT RESCUED ME

There's a version of success that looks beautiful from the outside but feels like suffocation on the inside. I spent my thirties collecting achievements like they were oxygen, convincing myself that being busy meant I mattered. But beneath the deadlines and dinners-for-one, I was grieving the life I hadn't made space for. The love I'd postponed. The moments I missed. The women I envied weren't always the ones with titles, they were the ones who looked... content. That's when I realised – success without balance isn't success. It's survival.

I used to think balance was something you earned. A reward for those who hustled hard enough. Achieved enough. Proved themselves enough. Like if I just climbed a little higher, ticked a few more boxes, then one day, I'd wake up and boom. Peace. Clarity. Maybe even a mortgage with a south-facing garden. But balance isn't something you earn. It's something you choose. And back then? I didn't choose it. I chose work.

Because work was where I knew who I was. I was smart there.

Useful. Respected. I got shit done. People listened to me. There were briefs, deadlines, budgets. Everything had a process. A structure. A plan. Life outside of work? That was messier. Greyer. No guaranteed outcomes. Just... possibility. And I didn't know what to do with that. So I buried myself in to-do lists and timelines, convincing myself I was building a life. But all I was really doing, was avoiding one.

I didn't have time for a life. Because work was my life. Monday to Friday, I was in the office by 9.30am and didn't leave until 9.30pm. Twelve hours a day. Five days a week. My desk chair had moulded to my shape. My Pret order was memorised by the staff. It was like Groundhog Day on caffeine. Relentless. Demanding. Gloriously structured – and I loved it. I thrived under pressure. I was doing big work. Important work. But I didn't realise the life I was building came at the cost of the one I was missing.

Until that dreaded day Samantha, my mentor, my friend, called me into her office. She rarely did that without warning. Usually, it was a calendar invite or a scribbled note on my desk. But this time, she just said, "*Got a minute?*" I walked in expecting to put out the latest fire or a client drama to contain. But she didn't open her laptop. She didn't even pick up a pen.

"The IVF worked," she said softly. *"Second time lucky. I'm pregnant. I'm going to take some time out."*

I blinked, smiled but looked back a little shocked. I didn't even realise she was having IVF. I waited for the business bit to follow. But it didn't.

"I've spent my whole life building this," she said, gesturing around her office. *"And I love it. But now... I want something more. I want a something I can call mine. I don't want to waste any more time."*

And in that moment, something shifted in me. Samantha had been my blueprint. Sharp. Polished. Unshakeable. And here she was, choosing softness. Choosing balance. Choosing herself.

I was in my mid-thirties. Still running. Still chasing. Still convincing myself that success looked like overflowing inboxes and well-behaved PowerPoint decks. And meanwhile, love had passed me by. So had quiet weekends. And maybe... the chance to build something beyond a business card.

Because how could I expect someone to choose me, when I hadn't even chosen myself?

That night, I went home and sat in silence. No Netflix. No wine. No emails. Just stillness. Just me. And I realised I was tired. Not just physically. But spiritually. Existentially. I'd been sprinting through life so fast; I hadn't noticed what I'd left behind. The dinners. The date nights. The quiet. The softness. All the tiny moments that make life worth living. So I handed in my resignation. No grand speech. No tears. Just a quiet goodbye.

The next morning, Samantha called me into her office. *"What's wrong Suki, is everything OK? Do you need a break, perhaps a holiday?*

I almost laughed. *"You're not listening to me, are you? I don't need a holiday. I need a life. Because this job... is my life. And I'm done with that life."*

Later that day, Michael, our MD, called me in. He was a man I truly respected. *"You know Samantha's leaving,"* he said. *"Now's the time we really need you to step up."*

I told him I'd already resigned. He didn't flinch. *"So what can we do to change your mind?"*

My voice didn't waver. *"I bring in twice the revenue of any other Group Account Director here, yet my team is half the size. I want more staff, and I get to choose them. I don't want to work past 6pm. On any day. And I want more money."*

He nodded. *"Give me until the end of the day."* By that afternoon, I had everything I'd asked for – two new hires, no more late nights, and a pay rise. So I stayed. And for a while... I had balance. Real balance.

Until we moved offices. And then came Julia.

The wife of a client, hired to take Samantha's place. Despite me doing the job. Despite clients loving me. Despite everyone knowing I was the natural choice. Julia and I clashed from day one. Her condescending tone. That high-pitched voice that sounded like nails being scratched on a blackboard. Her tendency to hover over your shoulder like a bad smell. She made my blood boil.

One day she called me into her office, sat me down and asked, *"Suki, do you know what marketing is?"* I'd been successfully doing this for over 10 years – was she really asking me this? My whole team sitting outside her office went quiet, waiting to see how I would react. I chose to take a deep breath and smile sweetly. *"Why don't you educate me, Julia?"* For the next thirty minutes she talked to me like I was a six-year-old.

Patience has never been my strong suit. When I could take no more, I told her I must go as I had a meeting. I lasted three months. Then I walked into Michael's office again. *"I'm done, Michael. And this time it's non-negotiable. You brought in some jumped-up bitch who couldn't do up her own shoelaces and I've had enough."* He didn't even argue with me this time.

The next day, Fiona, the Joint Managing Partner, called me into her office. *"Suki, we don't want to lose you. Hiring Julia was clearly the wrong call. What if we moved you away from her and gave you a seat on the board? You'd be the youngest Board Director of any top tier marketing agency. You could make a real difference from the top – you'd be great, you're a natural."*

I smiled. *"Fiona, because I respect you, I'll think about it. But know that my answer won't change. I've fallen out of love with this agency. And once you fall out of love... there's no going back."*

So I left. No job to go to. No plan. Just a suitcase full of experience and a deep knowing that I was done. Did I regret it? Some days. When I think about what I could've had. The kudos. The pay cheque. The power.

But mostly? No. Because that choice saved me. It gave me back my life. I worked less. Earned more. I started to breathe again.

The hardest part? Realising that maybe I'd learnt the lesson too late to get some things back. Not just time, but people. The kind of men I could have built a life with had moved on. And I didn't blame them. I hadn't made space for love. Not even for myself.

By the time I slowed down, the life I'd imagined had already changed shape.

But still I learnt. And from that day forward, I chose differently. I turned down more than I took on. I made time. I made peace. I began building a life that wasn't just successful – it was mine.

Maybe the lesson came late. But it still came.

* * *

THE LESSONS I CARRY WITH ME

1. ***Success can be a distraction:*** It's easy to convince yourself that being busy means you're building a life – but sometimes, you're just avoiding one.
2. ***Balance isn't given, it's taken:*** It won't fall into your lap once you've earned enough or climbed high enough. You have to demand it. Protect it. Prioritise it.
3. ***You can build an empire and still feel empty:*** Achievement without alignment isn't fulfilment. The quiet moments matter just as much as the loud ones.
4. ***Walking away isn't weakness:*** Sometimes, it's the strongest, bravest thing you can do. Especially when staying means abandoning yourself.
5. ***If you don't make space for life, life will make decisions for you:*** Time doesn't wait. Neither does love.

If there's one thing I know now: It's that burnout is not a badge of honour. It's a warning sign. I didn't need to prove anything. I just needed to stop running. And when I did, I finally had time to choose me.

10

THE GIRLS WHO FORGOT ME

Somewhere between being the fixer, the friend, the fighter, and the forever dependable one, I lost sight of who I actually was. Not all at once. Bit by bit. A slow erosion disguised as maturity. I wore the masks so well, I forgot what my real face looked like. Played roles so often, I forgot they weren't mine. And when I finally looked in the mirror, I saw a woman built entirely from shoulds and supposed to's. But none of it felt like me. That's when I realised – this wasn't just about breaking, it was about remembering. Finding the girl beneath the layers... and finally letting her breathe again.

They say when a woman turns forty, something shifts. There's this *zero fucks given* energy that creeps in quietly and then kicks the damn door off its hinges. And for me, it wasn't about rebellion. It was about revelation. My forties were the decade I wore every hat:

The people pleaser: I didn't know how to say no. I always put others first, even if it meant saying yes when everything inside me was screaming no. I mistook being liked for being loved. And I wore that smile so tightly, I forgot what it felt like to actually feel okay.

The fixer: Because that's who I'd always been. The one who made things better. Tidied the mess. Patched up the pain. I attracted men who needed fixing because that's all I'd ever known. Love as labour. Affection as effort. Confusing purpose with taking someone on as a project.

The endlessly loyal friend: The girl who cleared her diary in a heartbeat when her friends needed her. Who showed up when it wasn't convenient. Who listened for hours even when her own world was falling apart. I gave freely, thinking that's what love was. And maybe it is, but only when it's mutual.

The emotional paramedic: Always the strong one. The one you could lean on. The one who picked others up off the floor but never let herself fall. No one ever stopped to ask, *"Are you okay?"* And to be honest, I don't think I would have known how to answer if they had.

The tick-boxer: Chasing the list. Good job ✓ Good salary ✓ Good girl ✓. Living life like a checklist, thinking if I just completed enough tasks, I'd unlock happiness like it was some prize behind a locked door. But peace doesn't come wrapped in productivity. It comes when you put the pen down and actually start living.

The career woman: Polished. Efficient. Armed with a smile and strategy. I made it all look effortless, but behind the scenes

I was holding it all together with wine and self-doubt. My toxic trait? Being the woman who did everything for everyone *(without waiting to be asked)*. But never asking for help herself.

I wore them all so well, those hats, no one questioned them – not even me. But slowly, gently, and sometimes not-so-gently, I started taking them off. One by one. Because they no longer looked good on me. I started asking different questions. Not the ones I'd been taught to ask, not:

Will they choose me?
Am I enough?
Does this look right on paper?

No. I stopped chasing the checklist. I tore it up and binned it. Instead, I asked:

What are my deal-breakers?
What feels good?
What feels like truth?
What feels like freedom?
What feels like me?

And just like that, the way I made decisions began to change. I no longer filtered my choices through someone else's lens of approval. I filtered them through my own peace. If it didn't sit right in my gut, it didn't get in. I stopped waiting for permission to want what I wanted. And I stopped apologising for not wanting what everyone else did.

Because finally, I understood – I wasn't too much. Too complicated. Too ambitious. Too anything else. I was just too me for the wrong life.

It wasn't just habits I let go of, it was people too. Friendships that once felt like lifelines began to feel like anchors. I started noticing who clapped when I won, and who fell silent. Who reached out only when they needed something. Who gave just enough to keep me orbiting – never enough to feel truly held. It's funny how loud the absence of effort becomes once you stop making excuses for it. I'd love to say walking away was easy. That I packed up my boundaries and strolled off into the sunset. But truthfully? It broke me, every time, bit by bit.

Because they weren't strangers. They were the people I'd laughed with. Cried with. Did life with. The ones I thought I'd be talking to for the rest of my life. You don't just delete history like that. There were birthdays, brunches, and big belly laughs in the archives. But the breadcrumbs weren't enough anymore. I was starving for depth. For reciprocity. For connection that didn't come with caveats or competition.

So I walked away. Quietly. Without the drama. Just a soft exit marked by self-respect. And in the silence that followed, I didn't crumble. I expanded. Because sometimes losing people isn't a failure, it's a filter. A painful but necessary clearing that makes space for better.

And life, in all her mysterious grace, doesn't just take. She gives, too... once you're ready to receive. Because after walking away from the ones who only offered breadcrumbs, I slowly found my people. My tribe. Not just women, but men too. The kind of friendships that feel like a long, calm exhale. People who saw past the polished exterior, who didn't need me to be strong or funny or *together* to earn their loyalty. They just accepted me.

Flaws. Fire. And all.

We didn't need daily updates or check-ins. What we had was deeper. Grounded in honesty, humour, and the quiet comfort of being able to show up messy and still be met with love. They didn't flinch at the broken bits. They didn't shrink from the truth. And they never made me feel like I had to be smaller to make them comfortable. If anything, they expanded me. They reminded me who I was beneath the masks. They made room for the woman I was becoming. They made me better, not by fixing me, but by loving me as I healed.

Because sometimes, the people you meet later in life love you more wholly than the ones who've known you forever. Not because they've been there longer, but because they see the version of you that you fought so hard to become – and they honour her.

And that's the gift of your forties. You realise you don't need to wear every hat. Please every person. Prove every point. You just need to come home to yourself. It's not loud or dramatic. It's not some grand unveiling. It's a series of quiet decisions. Tiny shifts. Soft nos. Brave yeses. The courage to stop abandoning yourself in the name of being everything to everyone.

And when I finally let go of the girls who forgot me, the ones I'd created, the ones I'd clung to – I found the one who'd been waiting all along – *me*.

* * *

THE LESSONS I CARRY WITH ME

1. ***The hats we wear aren't who we are:*** You can play a role for years and still wake up one day and say, *"This no longer suits me."*
2. ***Friendships shouldn't be measured in history:*** They should be measured in how seen you feel. If you're always the giver, eventually you forget what being held feels like.
3. ***Acceptance isn't something you beg for:*** It's something you reclaim, the moment you stop needing approval to exist fully.
4. ***The right people won't require a performance:*** They'll love the you that's left when the lights go out.
5. ***You can't rewrite the past:*** But you can reintroduce yourself, as the woman who no longer plays herself to make others comfortable.

And one more truth: I forgot who I was, trying to be everything to everyone. It didn't happen in one moment. It happened in a thousand small ones. Every time I said yes when I meant no. Every time I stayed when I should have walked. Every time I made myself easier to love by becoming less of myself. I know better now. I choose better now. And I'll never abandon myself again to make someone else comfortable.

III

THE STORMS THAT SHAPED ME

Life didn't break me all at once. It took its time.

It came in waves. Betrayal. Loss. Death that came too close. People I thought would stay, didn't. Plans I thought were solid, weren't. There were days I couldn't get out of bed. Nights, I didn't recognise myself. I shattered, again and again. Not loudly. Quietly. While still showing up. Still smiling. Still pretending I was fine. And when everything was stripped away – the roles, the titles, the people, I was left with just me. No guide. No grace. Just the slow, brutal work of putting myself back together. Piece by piece. Alone. This wasn't healing. This was survival.

The storms didn't just shape me. They scorched me. And I still carry the burn. But I'm still standing. And I will forever wear those scars like armour.

11

THE PRETENCE THAT PROTECTED ME

There are moments that break you before you even realise you're broken. Days that start like any other but end with the shape of your world forever changed. They don't just mark time – they divide it. When truth arrives before anyone's ready to speak it, and you're forced to stay normal in a story that's anything but. That was the first time I understood what it meant to carry a secret that wasn't mine. Some sentences don't just deliver news, they shatter foundations. That's when you learn what it means to lose without permission. To cry in private. To smile in public. To keep living like everything's fine when nothing could be further from the truth.

I was a teenager before I saw the truth behind my parents' marriage. To the outside world, they were still together. Still under one roof. Still sharing a bed. Still performing the roles assigned to them. But behind closed doors, their relationship had long unravelled. I was sixteen when I truly clocked the shift. The subtle glances between my dad and another woman. The lingering conversations. The ease between them that felt far too familiar.

It was obvious, even then. I was a teenager with sharp eyes and sharper instincts. And I took an instant dislike to her. Not just because she was the other woman, but because she was also married to someone else – a gang leader, no less. She was a woman with no shame chasing someone else's husband. *My* dad was someone else's. *My mum's. Ours.*

No matter how many times she smiled at me or tried to butter me up, I wasn't interested. I didn't care if my parents were no longer in love. That wasn't the point. What mattered was respect. And she had none – flirting openly with my dad, right in front of my mum. She wasn't just breaking the rules, she was rewriting them, and not in a way any of us could survive.

She became the beginning of my dad's undoing. He loved her. Blindly. Stupidly. Wholeheartedly. But she? She was playing a game. Using him as leverage. Bait. Power. And that's when the real damage started.

It was a normal day. Nothing felt different. Until it did. There was a knock at the door. My grandmother screamed, sharp and guttural. I ran to the hallway, heart pounding, only to see her shouting at someone in distress. Confused, I tried to make sense of the chaos. A woman stood at the door – a reporter. She was holding a newspaper in her hand, waving it like a flag of war. *"What do you think about this story?"* she barked at sixteen-year-old me.

"What story?" I asked. And then she shoved the front page in my face. I stopped breathing.

The headline hit me first. Then the byline. Two men fighting over a woman. One allegedly trying to kill the other. My father's name in black and white. My father's face next to words like *assault* and *attempted murder.*

Suddenly everything made sense. The silence. His absence. The whispers. He hadn't come home because he was in a police cell. Along with the husband. Both being questioned over a crime that sounded more like a film plot than our real life. And there I was, sixteen, standing in the doorway of my family home, the truth delivered by a stranger with ink-stained fingers.

The trial went on for months. Dragged out. Pulled apart. She took to the stand and lied through her teeth. Said he chased her. Said she wanted nothing to do with him. Said it was all one-sided. She told the world she was innocent. We knew better. But truth doesn't always win in court.

Then came the day my world collapsed. I was walking down the street when I saw my cousin. He looked at me with those wide, sorry eyes and said the words that cracked something deep inside: *"Sorry sis, it's not good news. Your dad got ten years."* That was how I found out. Not from my mum or dad. Not from a phone call. But in the middle of the street, in daylight, with no warning. I nodded like he'd just given me the weather forecast. Like my insides weren't screaming. Then I walked home. Past neighbours. Past questions. Through the front door of a house full of people.

And still I didn't say a word. I walked upstairs. Shut the door. And finally let the tears fall, reminding myself – you don't break in public. You don't crumble where anyone can see. You carry it. You smile. You pretend. And when you're alone, you fall apart silently.

My aunt Cherry was the first to come upstairs. She'd been raised with the same teachings I had – that pain isn't public property, and tears are best kept behind closed doors. So, when she saw me, we didn't need words. We just cried. Together. Her presence softened the edges of my shock. Then came my uncle Taff. Steady. Grounded. Offering the kind of comfort only a man who's loved you since before you could speak can offer. He didn't say much, just sat with me. A strong shoulder. A safe place. Together, they tried their best to explain what had happened. But I was only sixteen, so they gave me the abridged version. Softened facts. Measured truths. Because somewhere deep down, even in their own grief, they believed I still needed protecting.

That night, I lay in bed asking questions to which I had no answers:

How had this happened?
How did he let this happen?
Why did she lie?
What would we do without him?

The kindest man I knew. The man who made sure I never went without. The one who always protected me – who was going to protect him now?

I didn't know what hurt more. That he was gone. Or that I wasn't allowed to talk about it. The weight of that silence settled in my chest like stone. People asked where he was. I lied. Said he was away. Said he was working. Said anything that sounded plausible. Because that's what you do when your life becomes the thing people whisper about. You protect the story. You play your part.

I don't remember what I wore to school the next day. But I remember how it felt. Walking into classrooms with the heaviest heart and the brightest smile. Like nothing had changed. Like my world hadn't shattered. They all knew, of course they did. My family were well known, and it was all over the news.

That's the thing about growing up in a family like mine – strength isn't just admired, it's expected. And on that day, my strength hardened. My silence sharpened. I became someone who could walk through fire and make it look like a stroll.

No one told me it was okay to grieve him. Because technically, he wasn't gone. Yet he was. The man who tucked me in. Who called me *"Princess."* Who never missed a parents' evening. He was gone. And in his place, there was silence. Shame. And stories I never wanted to tell.

I didn't know who I could talk to. So, I didn't. I journaled. Scribbled pain onto lined paper that soaked it up better than people ever could. The words didn't fix it, but they helped me survive it.

I stopped asking why and started learning how:

How to show up.

How to carry on.

How to perform strength when all I wanted to do was scream.

That was the day my softness began to retreat. I wasn't angry, not yet. But I was colder. Harder. Quieter. I became the girl who didn't flinch when people gossiped. Who held eye contact just long enough to make them uncomfortable. Who kept her chin up even when her world was crumbling.

Because that version of me? She was built to survive.

* * *

THE LESSONS I CARRY WITH ME

1. ***Some truths don't ask if you're ready:*** They arrive uninvited, unforgiving – and still, you have to find a way to breathe through them.
2. ***Silence can be louder than sorrow:*** It's where you learn to hold secrets that aren't yours and carry pain that didn't come with permission to speak.
3. ***When the safest person in your world disappears, so does your sense of home:*** You don't just miss them – you miss the version of yourself that felt protected by them.
4. ***Shame is a thief:*** It steals your right to speak. To be seen. To grieve out loud. And still, I held the story together like my life depended on it. Because sometimes silence is the only way you know how to stay loyal.
5. ***Looking strong isn't the same as being okay:*** I learned how to wear pain like it didn't weigh me down. Sharp. Composed, and tailored to hide the cracks, like a perfectly pressed shirt no one could see through.

Here's what I know now: Some chapters in your life come without warning. Just a headline. A knock at the door. And a life that will never be the same. That day changed me. And even though I didn't fall apart on the outside, inside I knew I would never be that girl again.

12

THE ME SHE GAVE BACK

She didn't come from me, but somehow, she gave me back to myself. In her arrival, I found a version of me I'd forgotten – softer, slower, and entirely present. I thought I would teach her. Guide her. Love her into the world. But it turns out, she taught me too. How to rest in joy. How to love without fear. How to be seen without earning it. She didn't need the strongest, most capable version of me. She needed the truest one. And in showing up for her, I finally showed up for myself.

They say Motherhood changes you. But no one tells you that you can become a mother without ever giving birth. That you can hold someone in your arms for the first time and feel something ancient awaken in you. That's what happened when she arrived – Maya. My niece. My first girl. The one who made me a mother.

She didn't come from my body, but she came straight for my heart. I always knew I was born to be a mother. I'd been doing it since I was a kid – looking after others, putting their needs before mine. But life had other plans for me, and I breezed through my twenties, thirties, and even my forties with men who never would've made the *'father'* cut. Still, the desire never left me. I just buried it somewhere deep, beneath ambition, independence, and practicality.

And then she arrived – proof that life finds another way to give you what your soul has always longed for. She arrived like the light I didn't even know I needed. She wasn't a distraction from anything missing – she was the beginning of something entirely new. A love that didn't arrive through partnership or passion, but through purity. Through presence.

She reminded me how to show up. How to love without needing to prove myself. She brought me joy – real joy. Not the fleeting kind. The kind that comes from tiny fingers wrapped around yours and a gaze that sees you without expectation. She didn't need me to be strong, or successful, or sorted. She just needed me to be there. And so I was.

She didn't arrive with fanfare or fuss. Just a tiny cry, a warm bundle, and eyes that would go on to undo me in the most unexpected ways. I still remember the rush – the moment my sister went into labour, we dropped everything and raced to the hospital, not wanting to miss a single moment. But in true Maya fashion, she was already calling the shots. We waited an entire day before she arrived – already on her own schedule, already showing hints of a strong-willed spirit.

And when she did eventually arrive, she was worth every second. Her eyes lit up every time I told her the story of that day, like she knew she'd been anticipated with a kind of love that didn't need explaining. She wasn't mine, not biologically. But emotionally? Spiritually? She became my first born.

By the time she came into the world, the cracks had already begun to show. I was spinning far too many plates. I was still holding on tight to everything around me, hoping something would keep me upright. But then she arrived. And something clicked. Not in a grand, movie-scene kind of way. But in a quiet, grounding way. Like my heart had been waiting for her all along, and now finally it could exhale.

She didn't need me to be healed. Or whole. She didn't need a perfect version of me. She just needed my presence. My arms. My eyes on hers. And something about that – about being needed in a way that wasn't transactional or performative, began to pull me back into myself.

I'd held so much for so long. Pressure. Responsibility. Expectation. But when I held her, it all softened. There were no deadlines. No roles to perform. No reputation to uphold. Just breath. Heartbeat. Connection. She taught me how to slow down. To be still. To find joy in smallness. In baby giggles. In first steps. In sleepy cuddles and milk-scented moments.

And with every smile she gave me, with every little hand that reached for mine, I found a little more of myself. What floored me most was how much of me I saw in her. The sass. The timing. The side-eye she perfected by age three. She had my attitude. My spark. And every time she threw a look or delivered a perfectly timed one-liner, my sister and I would exchange that silent glance – the one that says, '*That's definitely you*'.

She made me proud in ways I didn't know were possible. And she stayed close, every single day. Hearing her voice felt like the most beautiful melody. She'd call on her way to school and again on her way home. Every day. Without fail. Everyone who knew me knew what time it was – *'Maya time'*. She'd even manage to unlock her mum's phone while she was in the shower to call. Those calls were small pockets of joy threaded into my routine. Our own little ritual.

She reminded me of my own fire. And somehow, through her, I learned to love the very parts of myself I used to hide. She'd come and stay with me during the school holidays, and I became her London mum. Our days together were filled with silliness and structure, big chats and bigger cuddles. And if anyone dared say a bad word about me, she'd give them what for – *"Don't you dare say that about my Gil."*

I'll never forget the time she made fake wedding rings, from those furry pipe cleaners, for Marcus *(my then boyfriend)* and I. She wanted to officiate the marriage. Me standing there in my white dressing gown, Marcus made to wear a blazer with his joggers. Right after she uttered the words *"Dearly beloved we're gathered here to..."* she stopped, looked him dead in the eye and whispered menacingly *"you ever hurt my Gil, I'll find you and kill you." (LOL. she was twelve)*. She was fiercely loyal, my girl, and I loved her for it.

In those visits, I got to show up for her in the way I always dreamed of showing up for a child of my own, and she never once made me feel like I wasn't enough. Not the high-achieving woman who built agencies and relationships and identities out of grit. But the woman beneath all that. The one who just wanted to love and be loved without condition.

She gave me that. She gave me a mirror that didn't judge. I remember my mum scolding me every time I was acting like a brat *"When you become a mum, then you'll know the pain your words cause."* I used to shrug it off. But years later, when I heard those same sharp words come from Maya's mouth, they hit different. They hit home. Suddenly, I understood the weight behind my mother's words. And I apologised silently, knowing now what she had carried all those years.

Maya gave me back to me. She didn't fix everything – she didn't have to. But she reminded me that even when life falls apart, something new, something deeply good, can still begin. And maybe that's the point. You don't always rise from the wreckage alone. Sometimes, you're carried by a love you never saw coming.

Because while everything else was falling away, she arrived. Not to rescue me, but to return me. To remind me there was still something left to give. Still someone left to become. And just when I thought I had nothing left, she gave me the one thing I didn't know I needed – a reason to rebuild.

Love had arrived in the most unexpected form. Not romantic or idealised, but real. Solid. Daily. The kind of love that shows up on school runs and sleepovers, in silly selfies and sleepy phone calls. She didn't just soothe the ache – I hadn't even realised there was one until she filled it. She became my anchor. My calm. My reminder that I was still capable of deep, unconditional love, even if it didn't come dressed as partnership or marriage. This was a different kind of forever. A different kind of home. And it arrived exactly when I needed it most.

But life, as always, wasn't done unravelling. Because just when I began to breathe again, the collapse I couldn't outrun came for everything else.

* * *

THE LESSONS I CARRY WITH ME

1. ***You don't have to give birth to become a mother:*** Love doesn't ask for biology. It asks for presence. For showing up. For heart.
2. ***You can meet a version of yourself through someone else's eyes:*** And sometimes, that reflection is softer, kinder, and more honest than the one you see in your mirror.
3. ***When life delays one dream, it often delivers another:*** It might not arrive the way you imagined, but it'll be no less yours.
4. ***Children don't just inherit our features; they inherit our fire:*** And in watching them grow, we remember what's always lived inside us.
5. ***The words you once shrugged off will echo back through time:*** And suddenly, you'll understand your mother in a way you never did before.

And maybe my greatest lesson was this: I didn't know I needed saving. I didn't know I was still holding my breath. And then she arrived. She didn't ask me to be more. She didn't ask me to be healed. She just loved me. And loving her gave me back pieces of me I thought were lost for good. I didn't rescue her. She rescued me.

13

THE ME WHO WATCHED IT ALL BURN

There comes a moment when you realise, you're not just dropping balls – the whole damn circus has collapsed. You're the act. The tent. And the clean-up crew. That's what losing everything at once feels like. It's not a breakdown you can schedule. It's quiet. Exhausting. Invisible. You still smile. Still show up. But inside? You're slipping. Not loudly, just enough to know you're not okay. And the worst part? No one sees it. Because the strong one doesn't crumble – she just carries more. Until one day, she can't.

We don't talk enough about what happens when all three life pillars – work, love, and family, collapse at once. We're taught that if one is shaky, the other two will hold you up. If work is hard, lean on your relationship. If your relationship is unravelling, let the love of your friends and family steady you. But when all three go at once, there is no cushion. No backup. No lifeboat.

And that's exactly what happened to me.

Work had finally found its rhythm. After years of freelancing, I felt settled, balanced. Then John came into the picture. Brilliant. Bold. No time for nonsense. We clicked instantly. We'd both spent years helping other agencies thrive. It was time to build something of our own.

A breach at our old agency gave us the push we didn't know we were waiting for. Overnight, we launched a new agency. Our first client: an under-the-radar tech brand. Everything was hush-hush, but promising. We poured ourselves into it. Long nights. Relentless ambition. A shared vision. We turned a no-name product into a top three seller. We were even shortlisted for Newcomer Agency of the Year.

And then, without warning, it was gone. A new executive arrived. Smiled. Lied. Quietly replacing us with his own team. It didn't matter what we'd built. We were out. The agency folded. The dream dissolved.

At the same time, my relationship broke down. Joseph – the man from my past, the one I believed the universe had sent back to me, was no longer the man I wanted to build a future with. He arrived like a gift. He left like the harsh lesson he was.

And then came the final straw. A friend in need. A request for help. A financial favour I couldn't really afford but gave anyway. It took more than a decade to get that money back. And it cost me one of the most important friendships of my life.

Work. Love. Friendship. Gone.

I wasn't just overwhelmed. I was untethered. I didn't know who I was without the things I'd spent so long holding together. I felt like a failure in every direction.

When your whole life caves in, people ask the wrong questions:

They ask if you're okay.
They ask what happened.
They ask what you're going to do next.

But no one asks the real question – *Who are you now that everything that defined you is gone?*

I didn't have an answer. Because when I looked at my reflection, I didn't recognise the woman staring back at me. Not her tired eyes. Not her brittle smile. Not the way she couldn't fake strength anymore.

Up until that point, I'd built my identity on doing. Achieving. Proving. I was the fixer. The capable one. The one who always had a plan. The one who pulled herself, and everyone else, out of the fire. The friend who showed up. The girlfriend who poured. The professional who delivered. I knew how to hold it all. Until suddenly, I didn't.

And when the things I was known for disappeared. I felt exposed. Like I'd been wearing costumes my whole life and suddenly, I was standing in front of the world with nothing on. I realised how much of myself I'd wrapped up in being useful:

Without the agency, who was I?
Without the relationship, was I still lovable?
Without the friendship, was I still worth choosing?

I wasn't grieving a job. Or a man. Or a friend. I was grieving the scaffolding that had held up my sense of self. Because I didn't just lose things. I lost the roles I'd been performing. And those roles had become armour:

The high-functioning achiever.
The emotionally generous partner.
The dependable ride-or-die.
The woman who could carry everyone else's mess without letting her own show.

Strip those away and what's left?

Silence. Doubt. Grief for a version of you that no longer fits. A wardrobe full of clothes you no longer want to wear. A to-do list you don't care about. A future you can no longer see clearly.

That was the hardest part – accepting that I couldn't just pick up where I left off. There was no *'bouncing back'*. No neat comeback story. No timeline for getting it together. Because this wasn't burnout. It was a full-blown identity crisis. And no one teaches you how to survive that. No one hands you a handbook for rebuilding yourself from the inside out.

Instead, you sit in the wreckage. And for a while, you don't move. Because moving means making decisions. And decisions require energy. And when you're running on empty, even the smallest things feel impossible.

Breakdowns don't always announce themselves. They unfold in silence. I still got dressed. Still made plans. But my smile was hollow. My energy fractured. My joy, non-existent.

I stopped sleeping properly. Woke up with a weight in my chest that made even standing feel hard. My brain felt foggy, like I was living beneath water. I stared at my laptop, unsure what I was even good at anymore.

Rebuilding didn't start with vision boards or plans. It started with the basics. Making my bed. Taking a proper shower. Walking to the shop. Letting light back into the house. Not healing. Just surviving slightly better. I stopped pretending to be fine. But I didn't declare my struggle. I kept my circle small. Kept the performance low.

The clarity came slowly. In fragments. I saw how much I'd attached my value to usefulness. How I'd equated being needed with being loved. How I'd measured my worth through productivity and loyalty. I didn't know who I was becoming. But I knew who I no longer wanted to be:

The girl who held it all together.
The woman who never said no.
The friend who gave without pause.
The partner who shrunk to keep peace.
The professional who pushed through every warning sign.

So I didn't rebuild fast. Or publicly. I did it slowly. Privately. Without sharing timelines or lessons learned. And somewhere in the silence, I heard her. The version of me I hadn't met yet. Softer. Clearer. Braver. I used to think strength meant being able to hold it all. Now I know, sometimes, strength is knowing when to let go.

Let the tent fall. Let the act end. Let the applause fade. Because you were never meant to be the show, the scaffolding, and the safety net all at once.

The version of me who tried to hold everything together wasn't failing. She was exhausted. And maybe the collapse wasn't her end. Maybe it was the beginning of someone who no longer needed a stage to feel seen.

* * *

THE LESSONS I CARRY WITH ME

1. ***Holding it together is not the same as being okay:*** Strength isn't measured by what you carry. It's measured by how honest you're willing to be when it all becomes too much.
2. ***When everything collapses at once, it doesn't mean you've failed:*** Sometimes life strips it all away so you can finally meet yourself without all the noise.
3. ***People won't always notice your unravelling:*** But your body will. The ache. The fatigue. The numbness – that's your soul asking you to stop pretending.
4. ***You can be surrounded by people and still feel deeply alone:*** Especially when you've made a habit of showing up strong while falling apart in silence.
5. ***The roles we play become costumes we forget how to take off:*** But you are not what you do for others. You are who you are when no one is watching.

And here's the truth. Letting go isn't weakness. It's wisdom. It takes courage to stop clinging to what's crumbling and trust that what's meant to stay will. I didn't lose myself when everything burned. I let go of who I was pretending to be. I'm not rebuilding to prove anything this time. I'm rebuilding for me. No more stages. No more scaffolding. Just ground beneath my feet, and the slow, honest work of becoming someone I can live with. For the first time, that's more than enough.

14

WHEN LIFE ALMOST OUTRAN ME

I used to think the worst moments in life came to destroy us. But sometimes, they arrive to awaken us. To shake the ground beneath our feet so we finally stop running on autopilot. The day I almost lost my life, something bigger than fear cracked open inside me. Not just survival – but clarity. A knowing that I'd been living fast, but not full. Chasing, but not choosing. That crash didn't just break the car, it broke the illusion. And from the wreckage, I didn't just crawl out alive. I crawled out different. And that changed everything.

It started like any other morning. The kind you don't mark as significant until everything goes sideways. Music up. Thoughts ahead. Plans already forming.

I was on my way to the airport. Passport packed. Life waiting at the other end. Ten minutes from arrival. Ten minutes from normal.

Until fate rerouted everything.

I don't know why the car in front stopped. I just know every bone in my body whispered, "*swerve.*" At 65mph, instinct moves faster than thought. My hands reacted before my mind had the chance to catch up. I clipped the car. Another clipped me.

And then time stopped.

The world began to spin. Once. Twice. Round and round. From the third lane to the first. Glass rained. The inside blurred. Lights, Fabric. Motion – into streaks. The kind of spinning where everything slows, then folds in on itself. Where seconds stretch into silence and gravity forgets which way is down.

Somewhere between the spin and the stop, I felt them – my great-grandfather and my grandmother. Not in the car. Not in the flesh. But in the stillness. In the breath I didn't know I was holding. In the space that wrapped around me like a shield.

I couldn't see them. But I knew – they were there. Holding me steady in the chaos. Keeping me from falling apart when my senses had shattered. Sound. Sight. Gravity. Gone.

It was as if time paused just long enough for them to step in. To stand watch. To whisper, "*not yet.*" They held the space I couldn't hold for myself. They took the fear and held it back.

I've never believed in guardian angels the way people describe them – all wings, halos and heaven. But I've always believed in the ones I come from. The ones who come back. And in that moment, I knew – I was being carried.

I remember my last thought before the car finally hit the barrier and everything stopped – *'I'd die with too much left unsaid. Apologies I never made. Thank yous I kept meaning to say. I love yous I thought I had time to repeat'.*

And the arguments. The unresolved ones. The ones that ended in silence instead of softness. The ones where we let pride do the talking and let distance grow roots. If this was it, I'd be gone. But they'd be left behind. Left with the guilt. With words they couldn't take back. With no space left to make it right.

That's the cruellest part, isn't it? When someone dies mid-conflict. You carry the echo of that last fight for years.

Then came the stillness. A silence so complete, it felt like the world had been paused. I didn't know which way was up. I didn't even realise I was still breathing. It was only when I heard the voices. Strangers shouting, asking if I was okay, that it dawned on me – *I must still be alive.* The dead don't get asked if they need emergency services.

I was upside down. Dazed. But alive.

The SOS in my car had dialled emergency services. My body hadn't moved. My voice hadn't worked. But somehow, technology had stepped in where I couldn't. And when the words finally came, all I could manage was a single breath and one small answer – *"Yes."*

But in that moment, it felt like the most powerful thing I'd ever said. And just like that, I felt like I'd opened the doors back to life.

I remember wanting to close my eyes. To sleep. To drift into the quiet. But the voices pulled me back. Urgent. Kind. Anchoring.

I tried the door. Jammed. So I climbed out through the window. And someone was already there, waiting. An angel in a suit. Steadying me. Offering his hand like it was the most natural thing in the world.

People had stopped. Strangers. Humans with soft eyes and steady voices who saw someone in trouble – and stayed. They sat with me until the police and paramedics arrived. No fuss. Just compassion. In one short breath, my faith in humanity had been restored.

There was pain. Sharp and insistent. Running down my side like fire. But pain wasn't the loudest thing I felt. What overwhelmed me was gratitude. Dizzying, breath-stealing gratitude. For life. For breath. For strangers. For presence. For the chance to wake up to a world I almost left.

And in that moment, I knew exactly who to thank – my angels. My ancestors. I'd always believed they were watching over me. That day, they proved it.

I survived something most people don't walk away from. But I walked. Bruised, but walking. Straight into the back of an ambulance. Held by something far greater than luck.

Shock is a strange thing. It doesn't always arrive with tears or trembling. Sometimes, it shows up quietly, like fog rolling in. A stillness you can't shake. A strange sort of quiet that settles in your bones and makes everything feel like it's underwater.

That's how the next few hours felt. Like I was there, but not really there. Watching myself move through the scene like a character in a movie I couldn't pause or rewind. The flashing lights. The blur of uniforms. The warm hands checking for injury. The questions I answered automatically, like I was reading from a script someone else had written.

Everything felt distant. I'd slipped out of my body and left someone else to be brave for me.

I hadn't told anyone what had happened. Only my sister knew – and even then, just the basics. She was worried. I could hear it in her voice. Feel it in her silence. But I couldn't bear the thought of saying it out loud to anyone else yet. Because saying it meant it was real. And I wasn't ready for real. Not yet.

There's a strange guilt that comes with surviving. A heaviness that sits on your chest – not because you wish it had ended differently, but because you're still trying to understand why it didn't.

The drive home in my Uber was quiet. Not because there was nothing to say, but because there was too much. Too much to process. Too much to feel. What do you say after you've watched your life flash before your eyes and realised you weren't ready to let it go? That you still had things to say. People to love. Places to see. Promises to keep. I stared out of the window as the world passed by – ordinary and undisturbed. Shops still open. People still walking their dogs.

Nothing had changed. And yet everything had.

That's the strangest thing about surviving. The world doesn't pause to acknowledge it. But inside you, something deep has shifted. Quietly. Permanently.

That's when the tears came.

Quiet at first. Then uncontrollable. The kind that don't need sobs or sound – just a slow, steady release. For once, I didn't try to stop them. I just let them fall. Because in that stillness, I finally accepted the harsh truth – *I could have died. But somehow, I didn't.*

It wasn't just the accident that changed me. It was everything that followed. The silence. The what ifs. The slow, staggering realisation that life had handed me a second chance – and that not everyone gets one.

First, one of my best friends showed up with his wife and food. Then my dad and sisters, with care and concern.

One by one, they appeared. No fanfare. Just presence. Wanting to check I was okay – not because I said I wasn't, but because they knew I was well-versed in the art of pretending I was fine when I wasn't. They wanted to check for themselves.

They saw past the brave face. They always had. No one pressed for details. No one asked me to relive it. Instead, they brought what they knew I needed. Food. Laughter. Pyjamas. Soft things. Small comforts. Quiet kindness. A reminder of life.

They filled the silence without crowding it. They gave me space – while making sure I didn't feel alone in it.

I looked around and realised – these were my people. My constants. The ones who don't need an invitation to care. The ones who show up with your favourite snacks. Sit beside you without saying a word, and somehow make everything feel a little less broken. The ones who never wait for you to ask for help. Because they already know you won't.

The car was gone. The plans were paused. But what couldn't be replaced wasn't lost. Not really. Because in that wreckage, I found something sturdier than metal. I found purpose.

The days that followed were quiet but heavy. Filled with reflection. Promises whispered to myself about how I'd live. Who I'd love. What I'd let go of. What I'd stop postponing.

The tears didn't fall all at once. They came in quiet waves – the weight not just of what had happened, but of how easily everything could have ended.

I started holding people a little longer. Watching them more closely. Noticing the sun on my skin. The laughter of my nephews. The way my heart beat just a little louder in moments of stillness.

That kind of clarity comes at a cost. And it cost me the version of me that believed invincibility was protection.

There was also guilt. A kind I hadn't expected. For surviving when others haven't. For walking away when I could have been carried. For continuing on like life was normal – when I knew it never would be again.

Survivor's guilt doesn't scream. It whispers. It asks, *"Why you?"* And never waits for an answer.

I promised I'd stay positive. That I'd stop delaying the things that mattered. That I'd make space for joy. Ask for help when I needed it. Stop wasting energy on people who only take. That I'd measure success in presence – not performance. And that I'd be more careful with my words. Because when I thought my life was over, all I could think about was whether the people I loved knew. Whether they knew they were my last thought. Whether they could forgive the careless things I once said in anger.

Since then, I've lapsed. Of course I have. I've fallen back into busyness. Into people-pleasing. Into forgetting how fragile everything really is. But the memory always returns. A quiet reminder that life is not a guarantee. It's a gift.

And every time I hear my nephews' laugh. Or argue with my siblings over nothing. Or sit across from someone I love and feel completely present – I remember.

I remember that I walked out of that wreckage for a reason. And every day since, I've tried to live like someone who remembers that breath is borrowed. Time is fragile. And survival is never an accident.

* * *

THE LESSONS I CARRY WITH ME

1. ***You never forget the moment you think it's all over:*** But if you're lucky, that moment becomes the one that is the beginning of everything.
2. ***Love is what shows up when the crash fades:*** In food on doorsteps. In hands held without asking. In silence filled with presence.
3. ***Words matter:*** Especially the ones you might not get the chance to take back. Be careful to taste your words before you spit them out. Because once they leave your mouth, the damage is done.
4. ***Life doesn't wait. Neither should you:*** Book the flight. Say the thing. Make the change. Wear the dress. The promises you make to yourself after a near miss are sacred. Be true to them and yourself.
5. ***Detours aren't accidents:*** When you veer off course, the universe reroutes you to exactly where you're meant to be. Trust the journey.

The truth I came back with was this: I walked out of that wreckage alive. But not untouched. Not the same. I stopped believing there would always be time. Stopped believing I could run on empty, and it wouldn't catch me. Stopped pretending tomorrow was guaranteed. I still lapse. Still forget. Still get swept back into busy. But the memory is always there, waiting to pull me back. To remind me what matters. I didn't just survive that day. I was given the chance to choose differently. And every time I do, I honour the girl who almost didn't walk away.

15

WHAT GRIEF TAUGHT ME

Some losses don't just take the people you love – they take the version of you that existed before them. Some goodbyes aren't loud. They don't come with slammed doors or dramatic exits. Some arrive quietly. Wrapped in hospital sheets. Soft prayers. And the silence that follows a final breath. There's always a before and after to every goodbye. A quiet undoing that reshapes how you see the world, and how the world sees you. It changes you. Losing them didn't just break my heart. It changed its shape without asking. In grief, I found a kind of growth no celebration ever gave me.

Losing my great-grandparents felt like the world shifting under my feet. Not loudly. Not with sirens or drama. But with a slow, aching silence – the kind that creeps into your bones and takes up permanent residence. They were the bedrock of our family. A living example of what it meant to love deeply. Consistently. Without ego.

Their love was the kind that novels are too shy to write about.

Quiet. Unwavering. Stitched into the fabric of every day. They had been together since she was thirteen. Soulmates, in the truest, most grounded sense of the word. It wasn't performative. It wasn't plastered across Facebook. It was simple, steady, and sacred.

When my great-grandmother passed away, I watched a part of him leave with her. Not metaphorically – truly. Her absence hollowed him out. His eyes, once full of cheeky sparkle and storytelling mischief, dulled. His jokes lost their punchlines. His appetite waned. He wore his grief like an overcoat. Heavy. Constant. Inescapable.

At her funeral, he sat quietly, dignified as ever, holding it together, in the way strong men of his generation did. But just before we left the cemetery, he turned to her, calm and certain, and said, *"Don't worry, I'll be with you in six months."*

True to his word, exactly six months to the day – he was gone too. It wasn't dramatic. It wasn't sudden. It was as though his soul had been patiently waiting for the clock to run down. And when it did, he simply let go.

Their double absence was the first time I felt the true shape of grief. The kind that doesn't scream but settles quietly into your chest and makes a home there. It taught me that love – real, lifelong love, doesn't end with a heartbeat. It echoes. It leaves traces. And if you're lucky enough to witness it, like I was, it teaches you how to recognise the real thing when it finally comes knocking.

They were more than just elders. They were my roots. The early architects of who I was becoming.

My great-grandfather: The storyteller. The joker. The pillar.

My great-grandmother: The warmth. The matriarch. The one who ran our world with both softness and iron.

Their home was the safe haven. Their rituals were the language etched into our family.

Sundays at our house were sacred. The kettle was always on. The house always warm – not just in temperature, but in spirit. There was always laughter. Always leftovers. Always someone shouting to "*move out the way*" as plates piled up and the telly hummed in the background. We'd all crowd into the tiny front room, knees knocking, arms tangled, passing cups of fizzy pop and stories like they were currency.

It wasn't perfect, but it was ours.

My great-grandmother, when you watched her cook would say, *"Don't rush, or you'll burn it before it's ready."* At the time, I thought she was talking about the kheer *(Indian rice pudding)*. Now, I realise she was talking about life.

She had this way of looking at you, like she could see straight through to your soul. There were no secrets with her. You could walk into a room with a smile on your face and a storm in your heart, and she'd simply ask, *"What happened?"*

Like she already knew.

Like she always knew.

My great-grandfather? He was the mischief. The sparkle. He could make you laugh until your ribs ached. His favourite thing to do was make up stories. Ridiculous stories that made no sense but left you doubled over in hysterics. He had stories for days. Some real. Some wildly embellished. But he always told them like every word mattered.

When he left us, it was like the house dimmed. The lights still worked. The furniture stayed the same. But something was gone. The magic. The noise. The pulse.

And yet, the grief didn't destroy me. It grew me. Slowly. Painfully. But surely. It taught me:

To hold space for the things you can't change.

To honour the people who raised you in ways no one else ever could.

To appreciate the ordinary moments – because one day, they'll be the ones you long for.

Their legacy lives on in the way I check on people. In the way I tell stories. In the way I know, instinctively, when someone needs a hug more than advice. In the way I still sometimes hear their voices when I'm unsure of what to do next.

Then came the death of my grandmother. That grief struck deeper. She was the cloth that held everything together – the last one of my ancestors.

Watching her deteriorate slowly over the years felt like an ache you couldn't stop. A woman who once moved through life with strength and purpose now struggled with each day – each breath. Multiple strokes had left her paralysed down one side of her body. She hated asking for help. Hated the indignity of it. We all tried our best to help without making it feel like help. Her hospital stays became more frequent. More serious. And every time she bounced back, I convinced myself she always would.

But I still remember the last time – the final hospital stay, like it was yesterday.

I remember the words the doctor uttered to my dad. Words I'll never forget. *"Look, I understand you want to keep her alive and with you for as long as you can, but she's in a lot of pain. You need to do what's best for her."*

My dad simply said *"okay"*. And asked them to turn off the machine that had been keeping alive. He was devastated. Broken. But still composed. Held together by some invisible force, because everyone else around him needed him to be.

I didn't understand the weight of that decision, that composure, until I was asked the same thing, decades later, about my mum.

Losing my mum hit differently.

There are losses that take your past, and losses that steal your future. She was both. By the time we lost my mum, I was a fully-fledged adult. Rational. Responsible. Always holding things together. Always being '*the strong one*'. But all of that crumbled in the face of that moment. None of that mattered right then. In that moment, I wasn't strong. I was just a daughter who wanted her mum. What started off as a routine hospital visit turned into the darkest chapter of my life.

She was supposed to outlive us all. She was invincible, my mum. She had stuck two fingers up to three different cancers and walked back into life with a smile. She held on to life with both hands – celebrating everything, big and small. She loved loudly. Forgave easily. And showed up for people even when they didn't deserve it. Her love was an endless reservoir. I still don't know how she kept finding more to give.

The night before she went into hospital, I had stayed with a friend. I promised I'd be back to paint her nails the next day. It was her thing. At Christmas she always wanted the same colour (Merlot). I never imagined that promise would be the last one I wouldn't keep. My brother took her in, like he always did. We thought it was the usual six-month visit – another stoma blockage. Routine. Forgettable.

Until my brother called. I'll never forget the break in his voice – a sound I'd never heard before. "*Where are you?*" he asked.

"On my way back, why?"

"Come to the hospital – and pick Dad up on your way. The doctor said Mum needs emergency surgery."

When we arrived, the consultant's words were clinical, brutal *"Your mum's colon has been leaking into her stomach. We need to operate quickly. There's usually a fifteen percent survival rate, but given her age and health, it's unlikely she'll make it."*

My blood boiled. How dare he strip her of dignity like that? *"I'd thank you not to say this in front of my mum,"* I said, my voice steady but my heart shattering. *"She doesn't need to hear this right before her surgery."*

We signed the consent form. I walked her up to surgery, holding back the tears. My brothers words ringing in my ears *"OK mum, I'll see you when you come out."*

My tears betrayed me, sliding down even as I tried to be her strength. My mind raced with questions that burned holes in my heart:

What kind of daughter was I, not being there the night before?
Why didn't I paint her nails like I promised?
What if she didn't make it - would she think I didn't care?
When was the last time I told her I loved her?

The surgeon who took her in was different. Kind. Human. He sat with me and said, *"If we didn't believe this could help, we wouldn't be doing it."* I clung to those words. My mum was a survivor. She'd made it through everything before. She'd make it again.

She didn't make it.

No one prepares you for the grief of losing a parent. Not really. There's no manual. No timeline. There's just pain. Raw. Disorienting. Endless. There's guilt, too. So much guilt.

Could I have done more?
Noticed more?
Said more?

But here's the thing about grief – it isn't linear. It's circular.

Just when you think you've made peace with it, something happens. A scent. A song. A memory. Seeing a WhatsApp notification that says *'mum has left the group'* – and you're back on the floor. In tears. In pieces.

It changed me. Of course it did. Grief always does. But what I've come to learn is that grief and growth often arrive together. Not as friends – but as reluctant companions.
They don't ask for permission.
They don't follow rules.
They just occupy space.

They carve new space in you. And eventually, something else grows in that space. Something softer. Something stronger.

Losing them didn't just mark an end. It marked a beginning. Of understanding life in a deeper way. Of knowing what matters. Of learning how to carry love even when the people who gave it to you are gone.

If presence is measured in how long someone's love stays with you, then they are still here. In every soft word. Every fierce decision. Every quiet moment when I feel held, even when alone.

They were my goodbyes.

And they broke me and grew me in equal measures.

* * *

THE LESSONS I CARRY WITH ME

1. ***Real love doesn't vanish – it echoes:*** The people we lose show up in our habits. Our humour. Our instincts. Proof that presence doesn't need a pulse.
2. ***There's no guidebook for grief:*** It's messy. Circular. Wildly disobedient. It doesn't ask for logic or follow calendars. There is no closure. You just learn to make room for it.
3. ***Loss changes how you love:*** It softens you. Sharpens you. Makes you notice the small things. Hold people longer. Say *"I love you"* without delay.
4. ***You never outgrow needing your mum:*** No matter how adult you become, grief returns you to the child in you – the one who just wants her back.
5. ***Grief doesn't shrink – we grow around it:*** The ache stays, but so does our capacity to carry it. We stretch. We adapt. And somehow, we keep loving.

Here's the truth: I used to think grief ended with goodbye. But it doesn't. It folds itself into you. It lingers. It reshapes how you love. It teaches you how fast the people you need can vanish. How fragile time really is. I still catch myself reaching for the phone. I still ache at the moments they'll never see. I still carry them – not as wounds, but as a pulse beneath everything I do. They didn't leave me empty. They left me full. Of love. Of Pain. Of lessons. Of a story I'll keep writing, for all of us.

IV

ME BEFORE YOU, YOU AND YOU

Love. That four-letter word that taught me more about myself than any therapist ever could.

At times, I found myself in others. Other times, I lost myself there too.

I've been the girl who fell too fast. Gave too much. Stayed too long. I've written mental wedding vows over coffee dates. Cried over texts that never came.

But somewhere between fairytale fantasies and late-night heartbreaks, I realised – love isn't about finding someone to complete me. It's about finding someone who wants to meet me exactly where I am. Not in spite of my flaws, but because of them.

16

WHAT HE TOOK FROM ME

There's a kind of heartbreak that doesn't just hurt – it hardens. It teaches you that not all lessons come with kind hands. It doesn't just take your trust. It takes your softness. Your innocence. Your belief in the good in people. My first love didn't just leave me heartbroken, he left me altered. I walked in open-hearted and walked out guarded. It wasn't just my heart that shattered, it was the lens I saw love through. And the girl who came out the other side? She loved a little quieter, doubted a little more, and carried her own pieces like armour.

I saw him watching me from across the room. Our eyes met. We both smiled. It was innocent, just a flicker of recognition at first, but something lingered. That was the first time I noticed his smile.

He lived a few doors down from one of my friends, and like clockwork, every time I went to visit her, he'd magically appear. On his front step. Pretending to be surprised to see me. Like fate had a schedule and he was always on time.

Immy was five years older than me. He had this charm about him. Not the cocky, overconfident kind. The subtle kind. Quiet. Observant. Slightly mysterious. Like he knew something the rest of the world hadn't figured out yet. And the way he looked at me made me feel like I was the only person in the room.

At sixteen, that kind of attention is intoxicating. You think it's love. You think it's fate. You think you're the exception.

I'll never forget the day he finally found the courage to ask me out. He stood there, nerves barely masked with charm, and blurted out *"Can I take you out?"*

Without missing a beat, I replied, *"I'll think about it – but I'm not getting into your car."*

He laughed, nodding like he understood – until I suddenly spotted a family friend. Without thinking, I shouted over, *"Have you got the car keys? What are you waiting for? Get in!"* He just gave me that *'uh oh, this girl is going to be trouble'* look.

But somehow, that madness was just the beginning.

Before I knew it, we were in a relationship. And it was everything I'd imagined love would be – straight out of a Mills & Boon paperback. He made time for me. Complimented me. Took me out and introduced me to his friends and family. He even made me a mix tape. A proper cassette mix tape with handwritten labels and carefully chosen tracks that felt like a soundtrack to our beginning.

And I, a hopelessly romantic sixteen-year-old, painfully naive, thought I'd hit the jackpot.

He would show up with little gifts. Remember the smallest details. Drive by my house just to catch a glimpse of me. Call just to hear my voice. He made me feel special. Seen. Wanted. And that version of love, however fleeting, felt like the kind you see in the movies. The kind that makes everything else fade into the background.

I thought I'd found the one.

But love has a way of teaching you its toughest lessons when your guard is down. And Valentine's Day? That's when the truth arrived.

He showed up like everything was perfect. Smile on his face. Flowers in one hand, a beautifully wrapped gift in the other. I greeted him with a smile, lips stretched over the ache in my chest, pretending I didn't already know. Because I wanted to see if he'd tell me himself. If the boy I thought loved me could look me in the eye and lie.

He could. He did. For hours.

Eventually, I cracked. The anger. The betrayal. The disbelief – it all burst out of me in one sentence. *"When the fuck were you going to tell me?"*

He froze. The colour drained from his face. Then came the excuses. His mother wanted him to marry a girl she had chosen.

He was the eldest son. He couldn't go against her wishes. But he loved me. Couldn't live without me.

Classic Asian bullshit – dressed up as duty and love.

I didn't scream. I didn't fall apart. I asked him, very calmly, to take me home. And never contact me again.

That night, I went home, hit play on *Sinéad O'Connor's Nothing Compares 2 U* and cried. I hardly ate. I didn't sleep. I just... cried. Alone. For a week. Mourning not just the boy – but the version of myself that believed love could come wrapped in honesty.

I heard through the grapevine that he married a woman from Derby. I was happy for him. I packed away everything that reminded me of us into a small box. The mix tape. The letters. The memories. And left it to collect dust. I didn't need closure. I needed distance. I needed to remember who I was before he entered my world and made me question everything.

But life doesn't always let you move on in peace.

One day, there was a knock at the door. I opened it to find his sister standing there. Looking embarrassed she mouthed "*I'm sorry.*" Behind her, was a woman I'd never seen before. But the look in her eyes told me everything.

She was his wife.

She handed me a ring I'd once given him – now crushed in a vice. Bent and broken. Just like our relationship. "*Stay away from my husband,"* she screamed, her voice shaking with rage.

I stared at her, stunned. Not because of the accusation, but because of the sheer audacity. I hadn't seen or spoken to him since the day I walked away. I hadn't called. Texted. Nothing. He'd made his choice. I'd honoured it. *"You've got the wrong girl,"* I said, voice sharp with steel. *"If your marriage isn't working, that's on you. Don't stand on my doorstep looking for a scapegoat. I left him the moment I found out. Do yourself a favour, and don't ever make the mistake of knocking on my door again. Next time I won't be so nice."*

She left. And I felt nothing. Not anger. Not heartbreak. Just... emptiness. Like I was watching someone else's story unfold. Like I was a guest in a life I no longer recognised.

Later, I heard they divorced. Did I feel vindicated? No. It just confirmed what I already knew – he was never mine to keep. Just a chapter I had to close. A cautionary tale. A reminder. A man that didn't just take my trust. He took my softness. My belief that love should be like the books said it would. That if you gave enough. Loved enough. Stayed true enough, it would be returned in kind.

But sometimes, love is the first lie you're told. And your innocence is the cost. I carried that heartbreak with me for years. Not on the surface – you wouldn't know unless I told you.

But in the way I hesitated before trusting. In the way I flinched at certain promises. In the way I kept one hand on the exit, just in case. It took time to untangle myself from that pain. To realise that his betrayal wasn't a reflection of my worth – it was a reflection of his.

And still, I didn't break. I bent. I adjusted. I grew sharper. More cautious. More discerning.

The girl he left behind didn't disappear – she transformed.

And the version that emerged? She wouldn't fall for sweet words and borrowed promises again.

She'd been burned once. And once was one time too many.

* * *

THE LESSONS I CARRY WITH ME

1. ***Not every heartbreak leaves you tender:*** Some split you open just to show you how strong you are when you stitch yourself back together.
2. ***First love doesn't always teach you how to love:*** Sometimes it teaches you not to wait to be chosen; to never expect them to stay and what never to settle for again.
3. ***Betrayal doesn't always look like a knife:*** Sometimes it arrives with flowers – trust your gut, not the gift wrap.
4. ***Closure isn't something they give you:*** It's something you choose. Sometimes it's a box under your bed. Sometimes it's the quiet knowing you're done.
5. ***You can grieve someone and never want them back:*** Grief and growth can sit side by side – and you can honour both.

What my first love taught me: The girl who walked away from her first heartbreak didn't lose. She just learned to carry her softness more carefully, and to never again hand it to someone who hadn't earned it.

17

THE ME HE TRIED TO ERASE

There's a certain kind of man who doesn't fall in love with you – he falls in love with your spotlight. Your spark. Your shine. And the second he thinks he's got it; he starts dimming it. Not all at once. Just slowly enough that you don't notice it happening. Until one day, you catch your reflection and wonder who this girl is staring back at you. That's what Tariq did to me. He didn't storm in and destroy me. He made it look like devotion while erasing me piece by piece. And the worst part? He did it all while calling it love.

I met Tariq at uni, right in the middle of what I now call my armour era. Shoulders back. Walls up. Trust tightly zipped inside a *'don't fuck with me'* stare. I wasn't heartless. I just knew how to protect myself. Every night out brought a new contender – boys who tried to match my wit. My confidence. My refusal to shrink. Most failed within the first few minutes.

But then there was Tariq. From the moment he walked past, then doubled back. Looked me up and down, calm and unflinching. I knew he was different. He was cheeky. Unexpected. And exactly what I hadn't seen coming. Oddly, he didn't seem intimidated by me. If anything, he was intrigued. He was attracted to my confidence. My sharp tongue. My independence. At least, that's what he led me to believe.

What I didn't realise then is that narcissists don't chase women they see as weak. They chase the ones that make them feel powerful when they break them.

What followed was three and a half years in a relationship that taught me what manipulation in the name of love really looks like. Not dramatic or explosive. But quiet. Subtle. Eroding. Like rust. Like mould.

At first, it was intoxicating. Tariq knew how to charm me. He paid attention, complimented me often, showed up with thoughtful gestures and long conversations. It felt like something between fate and fantasy. But even in the early days, there were signs. Signs I sugar-coated, swept under the carpet.

He didn't like how many male friends I had. Not because I was flirtatious, but because he was threatened by their proximity. *"It's not the ones giving you attention,"* he'd say. *"It's the ones who see you every day. They're the ones you don't notice... but they're all waiting for their chance."* And just like that, I stopped seeing them. Not all at once. But gradually. One by one, I pulled away.

That's the thing with narcissists – they don't demand control. They make you believe it was all your idea.

He never shouted at me. He didn't have to. His words were lined with guilt, cloaked in charm. It wasn't jealousy, he said. It was love. It wasn't control, it was concern. He didn't want them to take advantage of me. He framed his insecurities as loyalty. Wrapped his possessiveness in poetry. And I, confident as I was, found myself shrinking to make him feel more secure.

It wasn't just one moment that cracked something open in me, it was the slow build. The constant hum of my intuition, getting louder with every red flag I tried to paint over in softer colours. Because by then, the signs had been screaming for a while.

There was the time we were walking down the street, nothing special, just a normal day. Apparently, some guy had looked at me. I hadn't noticed. I was mid-conversation, talking about something mundane. But Tariq stopped in his tracks. *"I saw that,"* he snapped. *"The way he looked at you."*

"What are you talking about?" I asked, genuinely confused.

He shook his head like I was insulting his intelligence. *"You can't even keep your fucking eyes to yourself when I'm with you. God knows what you're like when I'm not."* There was no logic to it. No truth. But I knew, in that moment, that it didn't matter what I said. He'd already made his mind up. And it only got worse.

One night we were out clubbing. Jags was there, the kind of boy who stopped women in their tracks because of the charm he exuded. There was an unspoken attraction between us, from the first day we met at uni, always had been. But it was one

I'd never acted on. Still, when we bumped into each other on the dance floor, just a brief hello, a passing exchange, I didn't think anything of it. I went one way, he went another. But Tariq had seen us talking. As soon as I was standing next to him, he exploded. *"So you're cheating on me now? Is that what we're doing?"*

I was stunned. *"What? No. You're making something out of nothing."* But once he was in that place, there was no talking him down. The rest of the night spiralled. We argued all the way home. Climbed into bed in silence, backs turned like strangers in a foreign land.

In the morning, he rolled over and smiled, like the events of the night before had been a figment of my imagination. *"I believe you,"* he said. That was the beauty of his manipulation – the way he could tear you apart at night and then kiss your forehead by morning. Like he was doing you a favour by forgiving a crime you didn't commit.

I didn't know what I liked anymore. What made me laugh. What I looked like when I wasn't tense. I'd spent so long walking on eggshells, I'd forgotten how to walk freely. I second-guessed every outfit. Every smile. Every sentence. My voice? Edited. My instincts? Ignored. My body? Policed.

But somewhere in the silence, I started to hear her. The old me. Not in full volume – more like a whisper. She was quieter now, but she hadn't disappeared. She was waiting. Watching. Willing me to come back to her.

The final straw wasn't explosive. It was quiet. I'd run a bath. Candles lit. Soft music on. Door locked. All I wanted was a little '*me time*', ten minutes of peace. I'd barely sunk into the water when there was a knock. "*What are you doing?*" he asked.

"*I'm having a bath,*" I answered, already annoyed.

Two minutes later, he picked the lock. Walked in. Smiled. Sat on the edge of the bathtub like it was the most normal thing in the world. And something inside me snapped.

Later that night, I couldn't hold it in any longer. "*I turn left, you're there. I turn right, you're there. I can't breathe. You live five minutes away, yet you haven't left my house in over a year. Please go back to yours. We need some space.*"

Shocked, he packed a bag. Left.

Fast forward... 3:30 a.m. Ding Dong. The doorbell rings. His car key had '*broken in the lock*'. He'd called the AA to get towed back to mine. Like it was nothing. Like my house was his home.

"*I'm going to bed,*" he said, walking behind me – into my bedroom like it was still his.

"*Not in here you're not,*" I replied. "*You know where the spare room is.*"

The next morning, I told him it was finally over. I couldn't do this anymore. I didn't want to do it anymore.

I wish I could say I walked away with my head held high, middle finger up, soundtrack blazing. But I didn't. I walked away exhausted. Anxious. Unrecognisable. Like someone had reached inside me and stolen something soft, something sacred. I didn't feel strong or empowered – I felt lost. Like I'd been living inside someone else's story, and now I had no script of my own.

I didn't cry that night. I just sat in the quiet and stared at nothing. I felt numb. Like grief – but without a body to bury.

The girl I was before him? She was gone. Not in the dramatic way, but in the quiet, creeping way that happens when you stop recognising your own reflection. I'd been accused so many times of things I hadn't done, I even started to doubt the innocent parts of myself. I didn't trust my instincts. I flinched at compliments and I always had my bag packed, ready to walk away.

But slowly, I came back to myself. I wore the red lipstick again. I played my music loud. I said no when I meant no, and yes when I meant yes. I looked in the mirror and saw someone wiser. Warmer. Still healing – but no longer hiding.

Tariq tried to erase me.

But I reappeared – like a phoenix rising from the ashes.

* * *

THE LESSONS I CARRY WITH ME

1. ***Love should never feel like possession:*** If it feels like control, it isn't love – it's toxicity wearing aftershave. Run.
2. ***You can be the strongest woman in the room and still find yourself in a relationship that erodes you:*** That doesn't make you weak – it makes you human.
3. ***Narcissists don't fall for who you are:*** They fall for who they think they can own. The woman that makes them feel most powerful.
4. ***You should never have to shrink to be loved:*** If you feel like you have to shrink for someone, they aren't loving you – they're editing you.
5. ***Love doesn't always come with bruises:*** Sometimes it comes with invisible scars. A quiet grief for the version of you it erased.

Everyone has a moment when the penny drops: Mine was that girl in the bath, the one who wanted ten minutes of peace and still couldn't have it. That was my line. The thing I couldn't come back from. That moment didn't just break the spell. It brought me back to myself. He tried to erase me. But I came back louder.

18

HE RESCUED ME, THEN RUINED ME

There are some people who enter your life like light through a crack. Gentle. Unexpected. Exactly when you need it. Joseph was that light. He showed me the kind of love that felt safe. Seen. Soft. But not every saviour is meant to stay. And sometimes, the ones who rescue you from the fire are the same ones who strike the final match. He found me twice. Loved me twice. And broke me twice. But the second time? That wasn't betrayal, it was betrayal dressed as home. The kind that leaves the deepest bruise.

They say timing is everything. Maybe that's why Joseph never stood a chance the first time round. Because he arrived when I was still with Tariq, buried in a relationship that was slowly starving me of self. At the time, I didn't even realise how much damage was being done. Until Joseph appeared.

We met at Selfridges, where we worked. I was a student. He was six years older, working full-time as a security guard. We locked eyes one day. Confidently walking up to me, he opens with, "*Are those eyes yours?*"

I laughed. *"No, I borrowed them from someone."* He roared with laughter, like I'd just told the best joke he'd ever heard.

I tried not to fall for him. Truly. I was loyal, even to the wrong person. But Joseph... he didn't just crack my armour, he melted it right off. He looked at me like I was the most beautiful woman on the planet, and I'd never had that before. Not like that. Not with such warmth and wonder.

He missed me when we weren't together. He said it, over and over. I struggled to say it back. He told me he loved me. I couldn't echo it, not because I didn't feel it, but because I didn't know how to say it. I was raised in a house where love was shown, not spoken. So I did what I knew best – I showed him. Even though I lived on the other side of London, I'd shop for him; fill his fridge; change the sheets, and do a quick spring clean, before heading back to mine. My love language was *acts of service*. His... *words of affirmation*. I think that's where I first learned that sometimes love needs translation.

Then came the day that changed everything. We were on the escalators at Oxford Circus. It was just us. People moving all around, but the moment felt suspended. *"Do you love me?"* he asked.

"What kind of silly question is that?" I replied.

"I want to hear you say it." He batted back.

"Don't do this, Joseph. You're putting me on the spot and it's making me really uncomfortable."

"If you don't say it, when we get to the bottom of the escalators, I'm going to walk one way and you the other, and you'll never see me again."

I thought he was joking, but my throat still closed. My heart pounded. I wanted to say it. God, I really wanted to. But the words were stuck in the way trauma tends to wrap around your vocal cords. I didn't say it. I couldn't say it. And just like that, I watched the man I loved walk out of my life.

I regretted it every day after that. He taught me the importance of emotional vulnerability, of saying things even when it's hard. Especially when it's hard.

Fifteen years passed. Then one day, out of nowhere, a message pinged into my Facebook inbox: *"You've still got the same eyes."* My heart caught in my throat. It was Joseph. I almost didn't respond. I don't believe in going backwards, but some people are more than history. Some people are unfinished chapters.

We started talking. The connection was instant, like no time had passed. He wasn't far, living close by and launching his own personal training centre. I had a background in marketing, so I helped. I threw myself into it – the branding, the design, the suppliers, the layout. I helped build his dream like it was mine too.

He still looked at me the same way, as if nothing had changed. Like I was still that girl with the borrowed eyes and the quiet armour. One night I took my best friend to see the space. I kissed him hello, slipped off my heels, and left them chatting.

When I returned, she looked at me and smiled – *"He's besotted. Couldn't stop looking at your shoes like you were going to magically pop out of them."* We laughed. I felt loved. Safe. Happy. The universe, I thought, had finally righted a wrong.

But the universe had other plans.

One month later, I logged in to check emails for the gym, something I did often. One caught my eye. It was from Sally – a client he'd recently mentioned many times. It should have felt harmless, but the subject line created a huge ball of anxiety in my stomach – *'Hearts on fire.'*

I opened the email. And there it was, in black and white. No confusion. *"I can't wait to be your fiancée."* Everything stopped. My lungs. My brain. My sense of reality. I forwarded the email to myself and to my best friend. *"Tell me I'm wrong. Tell me this bastard hasn't just proposed to another woman."*

I wasn't wrong.

He walked over to me like nothing had happened. Kissed my forehead. Rubbed my shoulders. The hairs on the back of my neck stood up. I told him I had an appointment. Left. I needed space. I needed a plan.

The next day, he showed up at mine. Calm. Normal. Like everything was fine. I on the other hand wanted to punch his lights out. He asked my opinion on something for the gym. That was it. That was the trigger. I turned to him and said, *"What does it matter what I think?"*

He looked confused. "*I care what you think. I love you.*"

I took a deep breath. "*Care about me? Love me? Is that a joke, Joseph? Why don't you ask Sally what she thinks? Surely her opinion is the only one that should matter to you? After all, you're going to spend the rest of your life with her.*"

The blood drained from his face. Silence.

"*Cat got your tongue?*" I asked. "*Did you really think I wouldn't find out? Are you that stupid? Your emails come to me. Now get up. Get out. Shut the door behind you. And don't ever make the mistake of coming back. I want nothing more to do with you. You are a despicable man, and I wish you had never walked back into my life.*"

He got up and walked out. I never looked back.

When it ends like that, it doesn't just break your heart. It breaks your reality. I felt duped. Ridiculous. How could I have fallen for the fantasy again? How did I not see it coming? I kept replaying every word. Every kiss. Every look. Trying to locate the lie. The shift. The moment I should've known.

But the worst part wasn't the betrayal. It was the ache that followed. Not an ache for him. An ache I couldn't name. An ache for the version of me that had finally softened again. Opened up again. Trusted again.

I didn't cry for him. I cried for me. For the girl who still believed in second chances. For the woman who let herself hope, even after everything. I cried because I felt foolish. Like love had played a trick on me and I was the punchline.

It wasn't just heartbreak. It was disorientation. A collapse of everything I thought I could trust. In him. In fate. In myself.

And beneath all of that? Rage. Not the fire-breathing kind. The kind that simmers in your bloodstream. Rage that I'd poured myself into him again. Emotionally. Physically. Financially. Rage that I'd helped him build something while he was busy building a life with someone else.

But more than anything, there was an ache I couldn't name. I mourned the girl I didn't recognise anymore. The softness I'd let return. The lightness in my laughter. The way I'd started to believe again. I missed her. And I hated that he had been the reason she came back, and the reason she vanished again.

I didn't want comfort. Or company. I wanted silence. I wanted stillness. I wanted to touch the very bottom of that ache and see what was left of me when I got there.

So I stopped dressing up the pain. I stopped trying to move on quickly. I let it sit beside me. I listened to what it had to say. I stopped asking *"Why me?"* and started whispering *"What now?"*

Joseph tried to contact me many times. Calls. Texts. Voicemails, they just kept coming, thick and fast. In the end, I changed my number. I never answered. Months later, I heard through the grapevine – he left Sally standing at the altar. No vows. No goodbye. Just vanished.

And that's when I truly understood he didn't betray me because I wasn't enough. He betrayed me because he didn't know how to love. Not properly. Not consistently. He couldn't even love himself.

Some people come into your life like light. But if they've never faced their own darkness... they'll keep dragging you into it.

And that's when the truth came.

He didn't ruin love.

He didn't ruin me.

He ruined himself.

* * *

THE LESSONS I CARRY WITH ME

1. ***Saying "I love you" isn't weakness. It's courage:*** But saving it for someone who deserves it? That's wisdom.
2. ***Pay attention to his actions, not his words:*** The man who looks at you like you're everything can still betray you like you're nothing.
3. ***Never confuse history for destiny:*** It didn't work for a reason. Some people are meant to stay gone, leave them where they belong... in your past.
4. ***Love shouldn't come with ultimatums:*** If someone threatens to leave unless you perform for them, let them walk.
5. ***When someone shows you who they are, believe them:*** Don't wait for them to explain and dupe you again. Fool me once, shame on you. Fool me twice, shame on me.

I'm left with this thought: Sometimes we need to repeat a mistake to learn. The woman who lets a man go a second time – she'll be unrecognisable from the first. I realised he could never ruin me. He may have ruined us, but he could never ruin me.

19

WHEN HOPE LEFT ME, BIT BY BIT

Hope doesn't always vanish, sometimes, it unravels. One man doesn't destroy it. Ten almost do. A string of sweet beginnings that all end the same. You don't stop believing overnight. You stop after every promise that wasn't kept. Every plan that disappeared. Every man who saw your light and still chose the dark. Bit by bit, I watched hope leave me. And one day I looked at my own heart and wondered – not if it was still open, but if you can truly save a heart that's been ruined, not by cruelty, but by hope. Because even the strongest heart can only be ruined by hope so many times.

After Tariq and Joseph, I needed some time out. Time to recalibrate. Time to find myself again. I thought a pause would be enough to reset the wiring. To come back softer. Wiser. Ready. But time doesn't mend what patterns repeat. What followed wasn't a heartbreak. It was a series of small cracks. Silent disappointments. And whispered goodbyes that eventually made me question whether I even believed in love anymore.

This isn't the story of one man who broke me. It's the story of many – each one taking something, until there was almost nothing left to take.

Sofian – The one I lost before I ever had him: We met on my 40th birthday in the South of France. He was everything I dreamt of. Lightly tanned skin. Effortless charm. A dangerously disarming smile. He looked like he belonged in a GQ spread – the kind you tear out and pin to your vision board, and spoke like he could charm a room full of CEOs and poets alike. Five languages. A property empire. A gentleness that made you forget your own name. I was smitten. We talked. Laughed. Connected. He gave me his number. Asked me to visit. But I was never able to reach him. Maybe I took the number down wrong. Maybe I didn't. He became the pedestal – perfect only because I never got to see his reality.

Marcus – The one I felt compelled to fix: An old school friend. Sweet on the surface, wounded underneath. He was angry at everything. At women. Life. Being let down by everyone. Nothing was ever his fault. So I stayed longer than I should have. I thought I could soften his edges. Fix the parts no one else had stayed long enough to soothe. But some men don't want healing. They want you to bleed beside them, even though you weren't the one that cut them. He didn't break me, but he reminded me that love isn't owed just because you tried.

Gavin – The one who chose the quiet life: An architect with loud shirts and quiet intentions. We spent six beautiful months together. Then Covid hit, and so did the distance. When we finally talked, he whispered, *"I want slippers. You want wings."*

That was all I needed to hear. He didn't try to shrink me. He just couldn't hold me. And that kind of mismatch hurts in its own way – not because they hurt you, but because they didn't try to keep you.

Daniel – The one who needed saving, not loving: A writer. Sharp. Intelligent. Tender. Quietly drowning. He wanted more from me than I was prepared to give. Time. Energy. Constant reassurance. I had always been honest – I liked what we had. Brief. Infrequent. Uncomplicated. But he kept pushing for more. And eventually, I realised I was trying to talk someone off a ledge they didn't want to come off. Love isn't CPR. It's not your job to save someone, and you can't revive someone who doesn't want to breathe on their own.

Walker – The almost who always lingered: Charming. Warm. Passionate. He made me feel like myself again. But he was in the middle of a messy divorce, and I knew I didn't want to be the rebound or the wreckage. So I stepped away. We stayed in touch – the kind of touch that always picks up where it left off. He reminded me that love could feel easy. But also, that timing isn't always on your side.

Martin – The one who warned me, and I didn't listen: A music composer. Creative. Soulful. Magnetic. We talked for hours. Laughed. Connected. But he told me early on – he wasn't ready. I heard him, but I still stayed. Because that's what hope does, it overrides logic. When someone tells you they're not ready, believe them. Otherwise, you end up performing for someone who never even took a seat. I learned that lesson the hard way.

Amir – The one who lit the match but wouldn't let it burn: An entrepreneur. Clever. Calculated. Dangerously charismatic. He was moving abroad; we both knew it couldn't work. But then business brought us back together and the chemistry was impossible to ignore. He had one foot in, one foot out. Always just enough to keep me hoping – never enough to let me move on. He was the spark that never became a fire – and silly me, I kept standing in the smoke, always mistaking it for a smoke signal.

Hugo – The one who chose fear over faith: He was kind. Thoughtful. Grounded. We had something real, until I told him I might be moving abroad. That's when he silently shut down. To him, I was a flight risk. He couldn't take the chance. And there it was again, that familiar ache of someone choosing the safer path over fighting for me. My heart cracked. Not because he was cruel, but because he was kind, and still didn't stay. So I left, like he said I would. But we became something else – friends. The real kind. The kind who shows up, not just when it's easy. He couldn't love me romantically, but he didn't abandon me. And somehow, in the echo of that disappointment, something purer formed. He broke my heart, then handed it back. Stitched together with honesty, and held by friendship. And I'll always be grateful for that.

Dean – The one who wanted to love me forever: He was ready. All in. Treated me like a queen. But I couldn't see a future with him – not because he wasn't a good man, but because I knew I would have to dim myself to fit into his world. We circled back and forth. I didn't want to hurt him, but I knew staying would. Walking away from someone good has its own kind of ache.

Jordan – The one who reminded me I could still connect: Witty. Brilliant. We shared a love of sarcasm and *Sex and the City*. He had a five-day rule I found charmingly ridiculous – and maybe a little sexy. I thought, even if nothing came of this, I'd found a friend. But the more we met, the more he pulled away. Hot. Cold. Lukewarm. Gone. And I was tired. Not of men. Of hope.

There were so many more. Each with their own lessons. Each taking another piece of my hope. There's a tiredness when you lose hope that doesn't announce itself with tears – just quiet disinterest. A tired that sits behind your eyes, even on your happiest days. The kind that makes you second-guess compliments, hold back texts, and rehearse indifference like it's your native tongue. I'd been here before, perched on the edge of maybe, and I was starting to forget what it felt like to believe in more than almost. What it felt like to be chosen. Completely. Without caveats or delays.

These men didn't destroy me. But they made me question whether love was still something I believed in. Not because they were awful – but because they all made me feel like I was never enough. And after a while, that's all it takes. Not one big betrayal. Just a slow undoing. A fading. A silence.

When hope left me, it didn't slam the door. It slipped quietly out the back – bit by bit, man by man. Until I stopped waiting by the window. I kept it closed, with the blinds down.

And yet, even after all of them – the almosts. The let-downs. The slow fade of hope, I was still that hopeless romantic who believed in love. Somewhere beneath the cynicism and the cracks, I still held out for the fairytale. And just when I thought I'd stopped believing altogether...

I met William.

But that story deserves its own chapter.

* * *

THE LESSONS I CARRY WITH ME

1. ***Hope doesn't break:*** It wears down – one excuse, one no-show, one almost at a time.
2. ***When someone tells you they are not ready, listen:*** Your heart is not a waiting room, stop treating it like one.
3. ***Chemistry sparks the flame. But compatibility is what keeps it burning:*** Longing stirs your soul, but it is not the same as being loved well.
4. ***Don't settle for breadcrumbs:*** Clarity is braver than pretending you're okay with less than you need. You deserve more.
5. ***You can be everything and still not be chosen:*** That is never about your worth or what you lack. It is about their vision and what they fail to see.

The truth is: You don't lose hope all at once. You lose it in moments. But you can grow it back, even from a single spark. I may have stopped waiting. But deep down, I never stopped believing. And that? That's what makes all the difference.

20

HE FELT LIKE HOME TO ME

He felt like home. Not in the way houses do, but in the way candlelight does. Warm. Glowing. Softly inviting. He looked at me like I was something precious, held me like I was breakable but worth the risk. A soft landing after a lifetime of almosts. For a moment, I believed I'd found what I'd been waiting for. Not perfection, just peace. The kind that wraps around you and says, "You can rest now." So I did. I let go. I softened. I believed. Maybe that's what makes it hurt the most – that I didn't see the storm coming, because it felt so much like shelter. He didn't just break my heart. He broke the part of me that believed I was finally done breaking.

I met William the way most of us do these days – swiping left and right *(mainly left)*. When his message landed in my inbox, I didn't reply straight away. His words were beautifully crafted, thoughtful in that rare kind of way that makes you sit up straighter. But he wasn't my usual type. However, by that point, I knew I had to do things differently. I wasn't looking for butterflies. I was looking for peace.

I'd been single for a while. Not in a lonely way – in a deliberate way. I'd spent years shedding the versions of myself that had come before. No, I wasn't the finished article. Who is? But I was close. Close to the woman I was always meant to be. One who didn't beg to be chosen. One who knew her worth.

I think there's something sacred about a love that finds you later in life. By then, the edges have been softened by grief, sharpened by lessons, and worn smooth by everything you thought was love but wasn't. You're no longer trying to be impressive. You're just trying to be understood, and accepted.

Eventually, I messaged him back. From the first hello, I knew he was different. The conversation flowed like we'd already known each other in another life. That first night, we talked for over three hours. As we were winding down, he said, *"I've really enjoyed this, Suki. Is this where you tell me you live a million miles away?"*

I smiled. *"Sixty-nine miles, to be precise. But who's counting?"*

"Damn it," he said. *"I knew it was too good to be true."*

I was half-asleep by then, but I still had some fight in me. *"Look, you can carry on dating mediocre in your catchment area, or you can step out of your catchment for something that might actually go somewhere. No pressure. Your call. But for now, I need my beauty sleep."*

By morning, his reply was waiting – *"I'm going to take you on a date. You know that, don't you?"*

I just grinned at my screen. *"I haven't agreed to that yet,"* I typed back.

The next week was a blur of messages and marathon phone calls. He wasn't just ticking my boxes – he was opening ones I'd padlocked shut. Sharp. Witty. Intelligent. Playful. And kind. The sort of kind that doesn't perform.

We had a date planned for the following Monday, but by Friday, neither of us could wait. *"I work for myself,"* I said. *"You do too. What's stopping us from grabbing lunch today?"*

"Nothing," he said. *"Let's do it."*

We met halfway. I tried not to get too excited – expectations are dangerous when you've worn disappointment like a second skin for so long. But the moment he arrived, I knew. There was an ease, a rhythm. We laughed. We flirted. The afternoon vanished in conversation.

Then, just as I was leaning into the moment, he looked up and said, *"I need to tell you something."*

There it was, that sinking feeling, in the pit of my stomach – the plot twist.

Was he married?

Was I the warm-up act before his real life resumed?

"I've got a date tonight," he said. *"We weren't supposed to meet until Monday."*

I laughed. *"Okay,"* I said calmly, almost relieved. *"Have fun."*

He stared at me, stunned. *"Are you serious? I've just had the best first date of my life. Do you really think I can go and meet someone else after this?"*

"I am serious," I said. *"She's probably been looking forward to this all week. She deserves the same consideration I would want."*

"I can't go," he replied. *"More to the point, I don't want to go. Help me craft a message to her."*

"I can't do that," I said. *"If you cancel, that's your decision. But don't involve me in hurting someone else. That doesn't sit well with me. That being said, I agree – this has been the best first date I've had in a long time. So, thank you."*

He cancelled. He stayed. And we spent the rest of the evening tangled in conversation and comfort. It felt like the beginning of something. Something real.

The next six months were magical. We spent most weekends together, marvelling at how lucky we were to have found each other after all the heartaches we'd endured. Fate had finally smiled down on us.

He told me I was the most precious thing in his life. One afternoon, curled up on the sofa and knowing how much my dad meant to me, he looked over and said, *"I can't wait to meet your dad. I want to ask him how I should look after you."*

And just like that, every wall I'd built – every steel beam of self-protection... crumbled.

He brought out a softness I didn't know I still had. I didn't just feel loved. I felt safe. Not in the way that needed protection, but in the way you feel when someone finally makes it easy to breathe.

He was chivalrous. He opened doors – all of them. House doors. Car doors. Emotional ones too. He'd carry my bags and say, *"I know you're strong. I know you can carry them. But can you just let me?"* And for once, I didn't argue. I let him. Because with William, I didn't have to prove anything. I could just be... until I couldn't.

Our weekend started like any other. I made dinner. He set the table. Poured the wine. And the conversation just flowed. But something felt off. We'd been out of sync for a few weeks. But for the first time, it didn't feel like an easy fix. We talked long into the night. Long. Raw. Circular. I felt exposed. My softness – the one he'd brought out, suddenly made me feel fragile. We eventually collapsed into bed, side by side, but galaxies apart. That night, the only company I had was my tears. Quiet, aching tears for a future I'd started to believe in.

The next morning, I packed my things. Ready to walk. But instead, we talked about taking a break. Just a month, to recalibrate. We had dinner that night like nothing had changed. But everything had.

I went home with a promise to reconvene in four weeks. I

thought time would bring clarity. What it brought was silence. Deafening silence. No texts. No calls. No us. That month was agony. I replayed everything. Questioned everything. Clung to the hope that love – real love, wouldn't vanish that easily.

But when we spoke, the space that was supposed to heal us had only hardened him. We couldn't talk. We couldn't listen. Every word became a misfired weapon.

And just like that, it was over.

Tariq shook me. Joseph broke me. But William? William crushed me.

William didn't just walk away. He evaporated. No explosion. No betrayal. Just silence where once there was everything. A man who once looked at me like I was the answer to every question suddenly had nothing left to ask.

And I... stupid, hopeful me – had bet on him. Not just for a chapter, but for the ending. I had folded up my fears, tucked them into his hands, and said, *I believe in us.* He didn't gently put them down. He dropped them from the greatest of heights and walked away, like I never existed.

And when it ended, it wasn't just grief I felt. It was something far worse – that deep, bone-level ache of being wrong. Of letting someone in. Again. Of believing. Again.

Because hope? Hope is a cruel thing when it doesn't come through. It doesn't break your heart like betrayal. It breaks it like trust. Quietly. Slowly. Until one day, you stop looking at love like a promise and start seeing it as a risk.

William didn't just end something beautiful. He ended the part of me that still believed in the fairytale. And maybe that's the saddest part – he didn't just take the future I pictured. He took the girl who still believed it could exist.

Because when he walked away, it didn't just feel like I was losing him. It felt like losing the version of me who had finally softened. The girl who still whispered *maybe*. The woman who still dared to believe that this time might be different.

And that was the real heartbreak. Not the man. Not even the ending. But the heartbreak of having hope. Real. Fragile. Reborn hope – and watching it get crushed under the weight of *almost* again.

So I let it go. Not just the man. But the fairytale. And maybe, finally, all the hope I had left in it.

William didn't ruin love. He didn't ruin me. He ruined the hope I had placed in him. But I have built altars from rubble before.

And I will again.

* * *

THE LESSONS I CARRY WITH ME

1. ***Hope can be the most dangerous thing we give:*** Because it doesn't shatter – it softens you first.
2. ***Sometimes home needs a new postcode:*** Just because someone felt like home doesn't mean that's where you were meant to stay.
3. ***There's a difference between being left and being let go of:*** One hurts your pride. The other breaks your soul.
4. ***Silence is still an answer:*** And sometimes, it is the clearest truth they can give you.
5. ***Grieving a relationship is bigger than the relationship:*** Grieving a man is one thing. Grieving the woman, you were with him? That's the real heartbreak.

What I know now is this: Those Brothers Grimm have a lot to answer for, filling our heads with fairytales so young we set our hearts on our own *'happy ever after'*. But they didn't tell us the whole truth. Not every love story gets the ending it deserves, no matter how magical the beginning. Some fade, not because it wasn't real, but because life had other plans. And that's the part that hurts the most – it can still give you everything you thought your heart had been waiting for, even if it doesn't last. I don't regret William. But sometimes I wish I'd walked away at the first hello. Because some endings don't just break you, they return you to your own beginning. And maybe that's exactly where you need to be, to start again.

V

SHE FINALLY BECAME ME

Not perfect. Not finished. But finally, fully mine. Belonging only to me.

For a long time, I dimmed my light. Not because I wanted to. Because I thought it made others more comfortable. Then one day, I stopped shrinking. I spoke louder. Dreamt bigger. Wore red lipstick at 10.00am, just because I bloody felt like it.

And now, here we are. Not flawless. Not always sure. But real. Finally liking the sound of my own voice.

Today, I'm not the girl I used to be. I'm not even the woman I thought I'd become.

I'm something better. I didn't just survive. I arrived. And it was worth the damn wait.

21

WHEN THE WORLD FINALLY MET ME

There comes a moment when you stop editing yourself to fit rooms that were never built for you. You stop softening your voice. Shrinking your dreams. Dressing down to make others feel taller. I didn't ask for space – I took it. I didn't wait for permission – I gave it to myself. And when the world finally met me, the real me, I didn't flinch. I owned it. Fully. Fiercely. Unapologetically. Because shrinking was never my destiny. Rising was. It was never about becoming someone else. It was about becoming someone I could recognise again. And once she arrived, there was no putting her back in the box.

For most of my life, I didn't fear failure, but I hated being seen in full. Because when people see you, they expect things. They measure you. Judge you. Want more from you. And for someone who had spent years flying under the radar, the idea of being seen felt terrifying.

But the truth is, I'd been visible the whole time – just for the wrong reasons:

For how well I could hold everyone else.
For how good I was at shrinking without making a scene.
For how perfectly I played the part.

So what changed? It wasn't the world. No. What changed was me. The day I stopped performing and started presenting. The day I realised I didn't need to be perfect, I just needed to be true to myself.

When the world finally met me, it didn't explode. But I did show up. Quietly. Gloriously. I shed a thousand versions of myself:
The quiet one.
The polite one.
The easy-to-love one.
The girl who made herself smaller in boardrooms.
The woman who apologised before she spoke.
The one who said *"I'm fine"* with a smile so believable, even she thought it was true.

I had worn so many skins:
The high achiever.
The peacekeeper.
The girl who cracked jokes when she wanted to cry.

Each one built for survival, not belonging. But when the world finally met me, I wasn't performing anymore – I was peeling. And underneath it all wasn't someone new. It was someone I'd buried to make others more comfortable. One truth at a time. One boundary at a time. Until I stood there, not new, but undeniably me. And let me tell you... it bloody felt brilliant.

I started taking up space with my voice. With my work. With the way I entered a room. I stopped apologising for being proud of myself. Not arrogant. Not loud. Just... undeniably here. Because I wasn't waiting to be chosen anymore. I had already chosen myself.

I spent years being the girl who made herself easier to love. I knew how to shrink in just the right places. How to dim my light so no one felt outshone. How to keep my brilliance tucked under self-deprecation and niceness, so I wouldn't be labelled *too much*. But I'm not her anymore.

The best thing I ever did was go quiet, not out of weakness, but because I finally realised my peace was louder than any explanation I could ever give. I no longer explain myself before I speak. I don't wait for the room to be ready. I walk in, as I am. Because I've learnt – being chosen is overrated when you've finally chosen yourself. I no longer sit on the edge of my life hoping someone will pull me in. I'm already inside. Feet up. Lighting candles. Pouring wine. This is my space now.

I started intentionally showing up as me – a red lip on a Monday. A *no* without an explanation. A decision made without asking twelve people for their opinion. I stopped asking, *"Is this okay?"* and started declaring, '*This is me*'.

And the wildest part? The moment I stopped performing, the world leaned in. Not because I was polished. But because I was real.

I carried that shift into every room I entered. Relationships.

Friendships. Work. No more playing small. No more pretending to *just be lucky to be here.* I earned my place. I belonged there.

I started speaking with authority – not arrogance, just certainty. I didn't soften my tone to make truths easier to hear. I didn't wrap my ambition in disclaimers. I said what I meant. I meant what I said. And I stopped asking people to clap for what I knew was brilliant.

I made decisions without waiting for validation. Pitched ideas I would've once kept in drafts. Shared thoughts I would've once swallowed. And when I walked into meetings, I walked in like I was supposed to be there – because I was.

I no longer showed up hoping to impress. I showed up knowing I had something to say.

Even in friendships, the shift was seismic. I stopped bending myself into availability. Stopped being the always-there, always-saying-yes friend, whose needs were secondary to everyone else's. I stopped explaining my boundaries like I was doing something wrong. I told myself "*No*" is a complete sentence. So is *"Not today."* And the ones who truly loved me? They never needed more than that.

And in love? That's where the shift felt sharpest. I used to be the girl who over-explained herself. Who softened her standards to stay likeable. Who tolerated crumbs and called it connection.

But not anymore.

Now, I was the girl who said, "*It's a no from me.*" Calmly. Clearly. Completely.

No second-guessing. No flinching. Not because I was bitter. But because I was finally done being the people pleaser. Done staying in conversations that didn't value me. Done pouring into hands that only left me empty. Done entertaining half-efforts wrapped in charm. Done mistaking attention for affection, and potential for partnership.

I learned to lay boundaries like a professional and stopped being impressed by mixed signals and mystery. I wanted clarity. Kindness. Consistency. And if a man couldn't offer that, he didn't get access to me. Simple.

Because choosing me meant I was no longer prepared to sit in the waiting room, hoping to be called next. I wasn't looking for someone to complete me. I was looking for someone who could meet me – fully.

And until then? I was whole on my own.

I used to worry I was too much. Now I know I was just too much for the wrong people.

Too loud for those addicted to silence.
Too bold for those who preferred women dim.
Too whole for people who only knew how to love in pieces.

But guess what? I'm not dialling it down anymore. I'm not rounding off my edges. I'm not hiding my shine so someone else can feel taller.

This is me. Unfiltered. Unedited. Untamed. I arrived in full, glorious Technicolor. Every scar. Every sparkle. Every sharp edge that once made me feel wrong. This wasn't reinvention. This was reclamation. And it was glorious. I'm not waiting for the world to give me a seat at the table. I built my own damn table. And I'm dancing on it in my favourite heels.

So, to anyone who ever told me to tone it down – here's my softest smile and my loudest "*no thanks.*" I didn't come this far to be palatable. I came to own my power. To take up space. Own my shine. Rewrite every rule I once followed.

I'm not just getting started. I've arrived.

This time, the world didn't get to name me. I named myself. And I said, *"Watch me rise."*

* * *

THE LESSONS I CARRY WITH ME

1. ***You don't owe anyone a softer version of yourself:*** The right people won't ask you to tone it down – they'll celebrate you for being you.
2. ***Saying 'no' without guilt is power:*** If it costs you your peace, it's already too expensive.
3. ***Boundaries aren't walls:*** They're doors with locks – and you're the one with the master key.
4. ***Your light will upset those who are committed to darkness:*** Shine anyway. Light the path. You were born to shine.
5. ***The most radical thing you can do is show up as yourself:*** Unedited. Unapologetic. Unmissable.

I remind myself every day: The world will always have something to say about how you should be. Softer. Smaller. Easier to love. But my life isn't an audition. I don't need approval to take up space. I need the courage to keep showing up as me. To stop shrinking myself for spaces I outgrew. And once I did? I knew I'd never trade that freedom just to make anyone else more comfortable again.

22

I STILL CHOOSE ME EVERY DAY

Even now, I have to choose me every day. Some days, I do it with bold lipstick and a power stance. Other days, I do it with shaky hands and tired eyes. Because even after everything – the rising. The reclaiming. The roaring. There are still moments I lose myself. In comfort. In old patterns. In trying to be enough. But I find my way back. I always do. Choosing you isn't a one-time decision. It's a daily act of devotion. A promise whispered, not shouted. You may falter. But you won't forget. Because this you – she's too hard-won to ever be lost again.

There's a myth that once you've arrived at your truest self, you stay there. That once you've reclaimed your voice, you never go quiet again. That once you've shed the old skins, they never find their way back.

But the truth? Some days, the old girls come knocking:

The people-pleaser.
The perfectionist.
The one who bends before she breaks.

But instead of locking the door, I've learned to let them in – not to stay, but to pass through. I pour them a glass of wine, hear what they have to say, then remind them who runs the show.

I've come to the stark realisation that being strong does not make you unshakeable. I'm now self-aware enough to know when I'm slipping – and strong enough to set the boundary that pulls me back in. I give myself grace on the down days. The duvet days. The doubt days. But I don't stay there. I set a timer. One day. Max. Then it's red lipstick. High heels. Power playlist. Head back in the game.

Because choosing me doesn't mean I never wobble. It means I've learned how to steady myself. To let my demons roam freely without letting them rewrite the script. It means I've built a life where I can bend without breaking.

And most of all? It means I never lose me for long. Not now. Not ever again. But I won't lie – sometimes, I miss her. The girl who believed love was simple. Who wore hope like perfume and trusted far too easily. She was soft. Wide-eyed. A little naive. But she was beautiful in her belief that things would work out in the end. That good people always stay. That love can fix what life broke.

Especially on the days when reality feels heavier than it should. When the grown-up me feels tired of being strong. Of always choosing growth. Of carrying the weight of knowing better.

But missing her doesn't mean I want her back. Because that version of me, as lovely as she was, didn't know how to say no without guilt. She didn't know how to walk away from things that hurt. How to stand up for herself without shaking. How to say "*I deserve more*" without questioning it afterward.

She lived in hope. I live in truth.

And truth, while not always easy, has saved me more times than hope ever did. That's the quiet ache of self-evolution. You don't just lose versions of yourself you outgrew. You mourn them. You hold funerals in the shower. Write eulogies on quiet walks home. Whisper thank you to the ghosts of the girls who kept you alive when you didn't know how to do it for yourself.

So, I've learned to carry them all with compassion. I let them walk beside me now – not ahead of me.

I nearly lost myself to convenience. To comfort. To the quiet safety of not trying too hard. But I've learned that staying connected to the truest version of yourself is a daily decision. Like choosing wine over cocktails. or heels over trainers. You have to do it with intention. Even when ease is more tempting than effort. Even when giving up feels gentler than holding on.

There are days when I regress. When I bite my tongue instead of speaking my mind. When I say "*I'm fine*" instead of "*I need help.*" When I scroll through my phone instead of feeling my feelings. And in those moments, the temptation to slip back into old armour is strong.

But the difference now? I notice. I notice when I disappear from myself.

And I come back. Every time.

The choosing. The showing up. The staying true – it takes effort. It's relentless, but it's worth it. Because I've learned the brutal cost of abandoning myself. How it chips away at your confidence. Your identity. Your joy. And I'm not willing to pay that price ever again.

Because healing doesn't mean you never fall back. It just means you know how to get up faster.

There is no final destination. No version of me that is forever safe from slipping. There is only the ongoing, everyday decision to not give up on myself. To keep reaching for the truest, fiercest, most honest version of me – even when she feels far away.

Even when it's tempting to be small. To be agreeable. To be invisible.

But I know what's on the other side of disappearing, and I'm not going back there. Not when I've fought this hard to be seen. Not when I've built this life brick by brick – with my bare hands and bruised heart.

So even on the days when I falter, I choose me. Even when I don't feel like it. Even when I want to hide. Even when the girls I've been before whisper, "*Come back to us.*" I raise a glass to them. I thank them for their service. And I keep walking.

Because this version of me? She's been clawed back from the

edge too many times to ever be lost again. She's not perfect. But she's present. And that, to me, is everything.

In the end, it's not about never losing yourself:

It's about choosing not to stay lost.

It's dragging yourself out of bed when your heart feels hollow.

It's wiping the mascara-stained mirror and daring to look yourself in the eye again.

It's telling the quiet lie in your head – the one that says *"you're not enough'"*– to *"shut up the fuck up and sit back down."*

It's not elegant. It's not poetic. Some days, it's survival with a side of red lipstick.

But it's yours. And you're still here.

Still standing. Still fighting. Still choosing.

And that? That's not a flex. That's nothing short of a miracle.

* * *

THE LESSONS I CARRY WITH ME

1. ***You don't outgrow your old selves by hating them:*** You thank them for getting you here – then politely show them the door.
2. ***Hope is a beautiful thing, hold onto it:*** But the truth will save you. Every time.
3. ***Healing isn't linear:*** Sometimes, it's one step forward and a spiral back. Choose you anyway.
4. ***Comfort is seductive:*** But ease can cost you everything you fought for. Don't confuse stillness with safety – peace takes work.
5. ***You'll never be immune to falling:*** But you can become fluent in rising.

What I unequivocally know now: I will not vanish quietly. Not after all this. Not after dragging myself back from places no one saw me disappear to. Some days, I'll fight with fire. Some days, with mascara-stained fingers and shaky breath. But fight, I will. Because this me? I earned her. And I will not lose her again.

23

TODAY SHE IS ME

I didn't find myself in the light – I was forged by fire, not burnt by it. I rose from my own wreckage. Ash in my lungs. Truth on my tongue. And wings I built in the dark. Through the ache, the endings, the quiet bravery of staying. Not perfect. Not finished. But finally, fully mine. After all the shrinking, the shedding, the surviving, I understand now – I don't belong to the past. The pain. Or the versions of me I left behind. I belong to me. I am not the girl I used to be. I'm not even the woman I thought I'd become. I'm something else entirely. Like a phoenix, I too rose from the ashes. And today? After everything... today she is me. And she was worth the burn.

To the woman reading this,

Whether you're seventeen or seventy – if you've ever lost yourself and fought like hell to find your way back, this is for you. And maybe... it's also for the girl I used to be. The one who thought shrinking was survival. Who softened her voice to be heard. Who twisted herself into shapes that didn't suit her soul.

You're not alone. You never were.

I wish I could sit beside you and say, "*I know. I know what it's like to forget your own magic. To trade power for peace. To live in hope that not only will someone choose you, they'll choose to stay the distance, to fight for you. To long for someone to see you – before you learn to see yourself.*"

But hear me now – the seeing starts here. With you. Choosing you. Not once, but every damn day.

There is a stillness I carry now. Not silence. Not absence. But a groundedness. A knowing.

Not because life has stopped trying me. It hasn't. Life still tests. Still tugs. Still tosses storms. But something is different now. *I* am different now. I don't fight the waves the same way. I don't drown in the same tides. I float. I rise. I swim through it.

Because this is what it means to arrive. Not to be finished. But to be full. Full of memory. Full of muscle. Full of lessons turned to instinct. Full of forgiveness I gave myself before anyone else. I used to think becoming meant finally being free of the girls I once was. But now I see them all in me. Not as burdens. Not as mistakes. But as bricks. As blood. As breath:

The girl who swallowed her words? She taught me what unspoken truth feels like in the body.

The one who loved too hard. Too fast. Too soon? She taught me how to keep my softness without giving it all away.

The one who begged to be chosen? She showed me what happens when you finally choose yourself.

I carry them all with me now. Not as wounds. But as wisdom.

There's a certain kind of beauty that comes after the breaking. The kind that's not afraid to be seen. That doesn't wait to be invited in. That doesn't shrink in the presence of power.

That *is* power.

This version of me doesn't tiptoe. She doesn't ask for space. She takes it. She isn't ashamed of her past. She honours it. She isn't afraid of being too much. She *is* much. And she's done apologising for it. She knows her fire. And she's not dimming it for anyone.

Today, I walk differently. Not just in posture. In energy. In intent. In ownership:

When I speak, I mean it.
When I say no, it echoes.
When I say yes, it's with every ounce of my being.

Because now, when I look in the mirror, I don't see someone trying to arrive. I see someone who *has*.

I earned this skin. I earned this voice. I earned this life. And no one gets to rewrite that.

So to every girl I used to be – thank you.

To every woman I almost became – I honour you.

To the version of me who walked through the fire. Ash-covered.

Shaking. And still chose to rise – this one's for you.

Today she is me. And like a phoenix, she rose. She was worth the burn.

And she is never going back in the box.

All my love,

Suki aka Azalea 💋

* * *

THE FINAL FIVE LESSONS I CARRY WITH ME

1. ***You don't rise by accident:*** You rise because you refuse to stay down – even when no one's watching.
2. ***The fire doesn't just burn you – it reveals you:*** What survives the burning is who you truly are.
3. ***You are the love you keep trying to earn:*** Be the home you once begged to be let into.
4. ***Self-worth isn't a finish line:*** It's a practice. A devotion. A choice you make quietly, daily.
5. ***Wholeness isn't being unscarred:*** It's standing tall, wearing those scars with pride and saying – this is me, and I'm still here to tell the tale.

Finally: Today she is me. And maybe, she is you too. Not despite everything, but because of it. And after every burn, every break, every becoming. I know this now. She was worth it. Every single step. Every single scar.

A FINAL NOTE

If you've made it this far, thank you – it means you stayed through the rising and the reckoning, the edges and the ache. Thank you for walking beside me through the quiet ache and the wild reclamation. For witnessing the girl I was, the girls I've been, and the woman I now call home.

Not every part of this journey was easy to share. But writing it down was a way of telling the truth to myself, too. Of saying – *you lived it, and you're still here to tell the tale.*

This wasn't just my story. *It was a mirror.* For the parts of you that needed remembering. Forgiving. Finally being seen. I didn't write this book to be understood. *I wrote it so you could feel understood.*

May you carry its pages like a compass when you forget your way.

May you come back to the chapters when the old ghosts visit.

And may you never again shrink for spaces too small to hold your brilliance.

You are allowed to evolve.

To rewrite.

To rise – over and over again.

And if nothing else, let this remain true – *you were always the heroine. You just needed reminding.*

With love, fire, and a sprinkle of defiance.

Today she is me.

And maybe... *she is you, too.*

About the Author

Azalea Tailor is a writer, brand builder, and serial survivor of life's plot twists. The big ones. The brutal ones. And the ones that almost broke her.

After a career spent building other peoples' stories, she finally stopped to write her own. *Becoming Her, Becoming Me* is her first book – a love letter to every woman who has ever lost herself. Whispered *enough.* Poured a large glass of wine. And started rewriting their story.

She lives by three things – truth, her friends and family, and good wine.

And if her words remind even one woman that it's never too late to begin again – then every scar, every sentence, was worth it. And she's done exactly what she came here to do.

You can connect with me on:

- https://todaysheis.me
- https://x.com/todaysheisme
- https://www.facebook.com/todaysheis.me
- https://www.instagram.com/todaysheis_me

Printed in Dunstable, United Kingdom

69005689R00119